# The Secret History of the Origin of Everything

—by Ed Schleicher

EDITED BY PROFESSOR BOTKIN SHADE
(B.A., B.S., M.A., AARP., Ph.D, Esq., AA., CIA)

A serial poem, by Sean Lause

ISBN: 978-81-19654-14-7

First Edition: 2024
Rs. 200/-

Cyberwit.net
HIG 45 Kaushambi Kunj, Kalindipuram
Allahabad - 211011 (U.P.) India
http://www.cyberwit.net
Tel: +(91) 9415091004
E-mail: info@cyberwit.net



Printed at Repro India Limited.

"Blunders are many, and none is more blunderful than man."

-Sophocles

**To my son, Chris, with love**

# Acknowledgement

I would like to thank Tom Beery and Will Wells, for their sound criticism and advice as I wrote this book.

Some of the poems in this book first appeared in the following literary journals:

"Such magic"---The Rising Phoenix Review

"The Christmas present"--Westward Quarterly

"Charlottesville'---Hawaii Pacific Review

---The Briar Cliff Review

"Make America Great Again"---Nationalism (Mis)understanding Donald Trump's Capitalism, Racism, Global Politics, International Trade and Media Wars (Mwanaka Media Publishing, 2019).

---Coal City Review

"Why no one remembers the name of Janet Leigh's character in Psycho"--

—The Bangalore Review

"The everyday randomness of grace"---Visions

"Death is a bad mechanic"---Poetry Super Highway

# Editor's Preface

To the gentle and loyal READER:

Two scriptures were recently uncovered. The first, *The Secret History of the Origin of Everything*, has proven quite controversial, since theologians and historians can locate no documentation whatsoever that Ed Schleicher III possessed any training in theology, history, political science, or any other professional field, nor any explanation why a man who claimed to be the direct son of God could have had two fathers of the same name before him. Nevertheless, his cult of followers, who refer to themselves as Eddites, has grown steadily in popularity and now has approximately ten million members. Ed Schleicher III died in 2016 due to apparently accidental self-immolation, but many members of his cult deny that he is dead and claim to have witnessed sightings of him around the country at various times. For some reason, these sightings tend to occur in used car lots.

Their messiah, then, is Ed Schleicher III. According to my own extensive research, Schleicher was born in Akron, Ohio, on August 6th, 1945. Nothing is known of his early years other than the fact that he appears to have spent some time as a tele-evangelist during the 1960's, during which time he insisted that the United States should destroy Russia, China, North Vietnam and California with a sneak nuclear attack. Ed later attributed his failure to bring about what he called "The Ha-Ha Armageddon" to the fact that in his sermons he had obviously though accidentally blurted out the secret plan on a number of occasions. His followers refer to themselves as Eddites. The religion—or cult—itself is known as Eddism. The name "Eddism" is said to be a portmanteau word, meaning "Ed" and "capitalism."

Schleicher's success came about because of the internet. He opened a small, conspiracy-laden website in 1995 and built it slowly into a multi-million-dollar business. The motto of the site reads: "Everything Connects—In Your Mind." Much of Schleicher's wealth came from marketing products on his website, where along with copies of his best-selling book, *The Secret History of the Origin of Everything,* numerous items emblazoned with his picture or his motto, "Better Ed than dead" were available for a modest donation to the "cause," what Schleicher named "Faith-based commercial initiatives." These include coffee mugs, beer mugs, sunglasses, pillows, t-shirts, sweaters, socks, jockstraps, emergency short wave radios, AR-15 rifles, hairpieces, and a special Ed-Energy drink, which has been proven to consist entirely of powder from superannuated bottles of Tang. However, for reasons shown later in this exegesis, copies of Schleicher's book became increasingly difficult to access over the years, both in hardcopy and internet formats. Another change in Schleicher's ministry was that as time passed less and less emphasis was placed on outdoor meetings and more and more emphasis was placed on social media, some of Schleicher's followers going so far as to develop a catch phrase: "If you don't tweet, admit defeat," a catch phrase Schleicher himself later claimed he was the first to coin and soon after copyrighted. The income from this copyright alone allowed Schleicher to purchase "God and Ed's Lear Jet" and "Ed and God's Helicopter."

Interestingly the main source of Schleicher's income –even more lucrative than his website— was his vast nametag industry. Each nametag is personally designed to include the follower's first name, followed by "IE: Ed." Furthermore, it is a key tenet of the Eddian faith that all knowledge can be reduced to nametags. Eddites are encouraged to avoid using their voices and indeed, to avoid any form of one-on-one human communication whatsoever. Text messages are to be the key form of communication when Eddites are in separate locations, but at first they also attempted to text message each other even when they met in person, and this led to various injuries and even fatal car crashes. So Ed issued a new edict specifying that when two Eddites happen to meet in person, they are encouraged to communicate by attaching various nametags to their persons and then removing one nametag at a time in order to explain themselves. This method at least allows them to keep one eye on the road, so to speak.

Eddites refer to this process as "Naming and Nailing," or sometimes as "Word Crucifixions." Eddites have been known to chant this mantra to themselves: "Name it and nail it, you won't bewail it." Nevertheless, this practice has led to some difficulties, as Eddites are often seen in public driving entire truckloads of nametags, even going so far as to wear nametags in their hair in order to possess sufficient words for everyday communication. Eddites believe that through the use of nametags alone they can identify and define any person, place, thing, idea, situation, or political, social, philosophical or religious reality. This practice accords with one of the key Eddite scriptures: "Clarity and precision in public discourse is Godly and Edly." Thousands of Eddites make their living in the nametag industry. Moreover, Eddites can be readily identified in public because they rarely leave home unless covered from neck to toes with what they call "Generic Nametags", in order to engage in informal, everyday conversations. Some examples of these nametags —include: "How ya doin?" "Hot enough for ya?" "It's not the heat it's the humidity," "I heard that!" "Have a blessed day," "Have a good one," "Well bless your heart," "Same old, same old," "It's goin'" "Omagod," "How about them...(fill in sports team), "LOL" and "Yipper!"

Apparently, as it were, this seeming obsession with nametags is connected in turn to the so-called "Eddian Doctrine on the Necessity of Censorship." It appears that according to this doctrine, since each of us is named before we can ever speak, it therefore logically follows that we should not be permitted to speak until we have been properly identified with a nametag. Furthermore, if one's nametag might imply that one might, if left "uncorrected," speak or write words that might potentially contradict scripture or represent a threat to the coherence of social beliefs, then one may be legally censored or even imprisoned.

One Eddite was excommunicated merely for sending his mother a Mother's Day card informing her that unless she converts to Eddism, she is destined for Hell. This was considered somewhat harsh even by Eddite standards, plus Eddites only send Mother's Day text-messages. Greeting cards are seen as profane.

A best-selling author may seem to be an unlikely candidate for a bibliophobe, but in fact several years ago, when Schleicher was investigated by the IRS for possible tax fraud related to his lost marble collection, and by the MLA on a pernicious charge of plagiarism, he ordered this his followers return all their copies of his book to him, with full refunds. Apparently the original text of the scripture may have contained a reference to the Pete Best Fan Club Schleicher began in 1962 and which appears to have lost money. There is no evidence the refunds were ever provided, but the Eddites loyally returned all their copies of the book, and until this particular find and its re-printing by this editor, all copies of the Eddite bible were believed to have been lost to history, since Schleicher appears to have burned all copies of his book, not merely it is believed, out of a desire to suppress evidence he did not want the government to see but also from a seemingly uncontrollable desire to burn books. On numerous occasions in his past, Schleicher was spotted in courts all over the country answering charges of vandalism and arson. He was known to have attempted to burn books at garage sales, inside libraries, and was even known to sneak up on readers from behind in public and set their books on fire using a Zippo lighter. It has been speculated, in fact, that Schleicher's intellectual form of pyromania may have been the key factor in his death, since one alleged eyewitness to this curious behavior of Schleicher's claims that after burning down a local book sale, Schleicher suddenly noticed all the nametags on his own person and instinctively, or unthinkingly, or perhaps even joyfully, set fire to himself.

However, Schleicher's unfortunate self-immolation inspired his followers, ever zealous, Courteous Reader, to imitate his zeal, and they proceeded to imitate his noble if highly flammable protest into a passion for burning. Their particular zeal appears (if facts cannot be discounted as mere theories or worse, blind rumor) to have vented its righteous passion on public buildings, starting with city halls, state capitol buildings, then moving up the hierarchy to burn down the entire Library of Congress. Once their holy fervor was sufficiently aroused, they moved on to private structures, such as their neighbors' houses, garages and boats. The most noted of these flamtagenates was Gerald Gardyloo, who insisted that doghouses represent a restraint on the freedoms of venerable quadrupeds. Unfortunately for the tragic Mr. Gardyloo, his personal mission came to an enlightening end when, while attempting to set fire to a neighbor's doghouse, he accidentally set fire to its occupant, a Tasmanian bulldog. The terrified beast promptly embedded its huge molars into a not-to-be-mentioned portion of Gardyloo's anatomy, and both beast and saint were reduced to ashes. Unable to distinguish which of the victims' ashes belonged to whose previous owner, a group of loyal Eddites, knowing of Gardyloo's quest to free all canines, scooped up the entire pile of remains and buried it in a local pet cemetery.

The difficulty of acquiring an extant text of *The Secret History* was exacerbated by Schleicher's previously-mentioned and highly eccentric view of the danger of individual words. In fact, Schleicher's apparent obsession with censorship appears to have begun early in his career. One day he suddenly announced on his website that from this day forth, all his followers were prohibited from speaking or writing pronouns. This proved troublesome to some, but unfortunately Schleicher only made matters worse when he subsequently announced that his followers were also prohibited from using articles, prepositions, any word beginning with the prefix "trans," and finally, any word beginning with the letter "F" (1).

The degree to which this practice of censorship appears to have gotten somewhat out of hand can be seen in the fact that before long, regular library patrons began noticing that when they attempted to look up the meaning of a word in the dictionary, many of the words themselves had been either blacked out with a Sharpie or in some cases even cut from the page entirely with a pair of scissors or perhaps a razor concealed about the person of a previous "reader" who was most likely an Eddite. Coincident with these admittedly unusual phenomena, museum patrons began to notice that naked statues had certain body parts blacked over with a Sharpie or a crayon, and in other cases tthe same offending body part was found to be covered with a photograph of Nancy Reagan.

Schleicher's strict practice of language-control, unfortunately, he also applied to his scriptures, with the result that all internet copies of *The Secret History of the Origin of Everything* were soon nearly impossible to read and comprehend. Many passages to this day are fiercely debated among religious scholars. There is even a rogue or "gnostic" version of the book—included in this volume—that presents a radically different interpretation of Schleicher's ministry. This text, *The Real History of Ed,* was clearly written by someone other than Schleicher and is not really a scripture at all but a kind of counter-text of the kind once called "satire," before that particular genre faded from view after the death of irony (2). One example of the difference between the two narratives is that while Schleicher himself claims to have miraculously fed thousands of his hungry followers with a handful of fish, the gnostic text claims that he did this by holding up a "Captain D's" restaurant with a .45 automatic.

The only known remaining copy of Schleicher's book—which thankfully (for the purpose of historical preservation) the reader now holds in his/him/her/hers/their/our/your hands or is reading online without the need for touch, scent, or texture—was recovered in the remains of a lending library in Winesburg, Ohio. Contrary to internet claims, it appears that Schleicher himself was not directly responsible for this arson. Rather, he appears to have been attempting to burn a small pile of books about the Holocaust when he accidentally set fire to half of

Shawnee Valley, resulting in the great Shawnee Forest Fire of 2008, which devastated seventeen hundred and seventy six square miles of wilderness and, somewhat remarkably, ended by heading straight for the Winesburg Public Library and burning it to the ground. Fortunately, no one was killed in the fire. Interestingly, only two books were found in the smoldering ruins of the library—*The Secret History of the Origin of Everything,* and *My Friend, Flicka.*

The book you now hold in your hands (or your virtual hands, if you are reading online) is the only official text, and the most juried text (by the editor himself) available of this now rare religious document. A variant text, *The Real History of Ed*, as noted, has been demonstrably proven to be a fraud and a forgery, a point I will come back to again and again, not only because of its farcical inaccuracy, but because its cowardly, anonymous author has shown the utter temerity of referring to this editor—a widely published and respected member of the cognoscenti, as "crazy as fifty monkeys in a sack." In fact, this corrupted and corrupt text appears to be little more than a bit of toothless satire penned by some witty wag with too much leisure time on his hands. For instance, he claims that his book is actually Gnostic in origin, and was uncovered outside a village in Egypt, not Nag Hammadi, but rather Nag Yomama, and that this new "Gnostic" scripture was suppressed by Eddite religious authorities because of the dangerous truths it contains. A diligent search on Google Maps revealed no such town as Nag Yomama to be in existence. However, for the sake of historical accuracy, selections from this text are included here in footnotes, just as a sign to the reader of how the Eddite faith has already stirred international controversy, along with scurrilous defamations.

A Brief Digression on How to Read This Book: Given the profound depths of this Editor's thought and commentary, he is aware that sections of this critical guide may prove difficult to read and comprehend, especially among the illiterate. Therefore, I perpend the following brief guide to perusing the contents of my guide:

1 First and foremost, I recommend reading each word slowly and carefully, employing the optical method of moving one's eyes smoothly across the page from izquierda to de recho. However, this method does not preclude the possibility of the reader suffering from temporary Strabisimus, due to the many paradoxes embedded in the text. To preclude such an unfortunate event, this author further recommends that the reader employ two simple electrical clamps, one attached to the side of each eye, so that if one begins to shift outside its usual position inside its socket, said reader may adjust to the motion merely by giving a hard tug to that specific orb until the iris returns to its appropriate homeostatic state.

2 Second, be sure to study each footnote carefully, granting it a minimum of twelve intense readings before moving on to the two scriptures themselves. Read the most inspired and inspiring passages out loud before committing them to memory. Do not hesitate, moreover, to immolate your laptop if your domicile is invaded by the Deep State or local PTA.

3 Third, due to the renowned honesty, clarity and openness of thought duly ascribed to this editor, the reader may best comprehend the purity of my prose by reading it in a location that best approximates the state of the text itself. Therefore, the most determined reader is advised to read this book while standing in the middle of the town square of his choice, stark naked. Furthermore, since the revelations contained within this tractatus may have the effect of turning his present views of the world topsy-turvy, it may prove expeditious to read the more complex, ambiguous, and startling sections while hanging naked upside-down from the steeple of the nearest church.

4 Fourth, and most pendently, this editor has at times felt compelled, in judicious search for originality, to make use of certain words not according to their mundane dictionary definitions, but rather according to the much more fertile digressions of his imagination, vis-à-vis, the powerful zeal of his utterance. As a case in point, I refer my Courteous

Reader to my unique employment of the above word, "pendently," the word "pendent" now commonly used by certain postmodern novelists to mean whatever they choose it to mean, and in such a manner as to convince said reader of the vast extent of his vocabulary. In a similar vein, I have been known to use the terms "nauseous" and "nauseated" interchangeably, after demotic vernacular, to describe my physical reaction to high speed vehicular car chases.

5 Fifth, the careful reader will take note of my frequent use of mystical *types* and *symbols*, which like the work of certain postmodern poets, the reader may be relieved of the burden of independent thought so as to learn the key revelation that a poet's words may be taken to refer to whatever that inventive reader may himself choose them to mean, leading to many creative interpretations of texts, not to mention tenure. However, this fact does not preclude the pendent possibility that my specific types and images do not refer, in any given linguistic circumstance, to ABSOLUTE TRUTHS which should not be questioned or doubted by the reader upon penalty of lawsuit, and that furthermore, as with many a contemporary poet, this same reader kindly show this author the due respect of at least entertaining the possibility that I never come closer to the root truth of things than when I have no idea what I am talking about.

As an example, whenever the reader, while perusing this treatise, stumbles across a penis, it is to be inferred that I am referring to an abstract concept, in this particular case, the American ECONOMY, and furthermore, since I am reluctant to offend the delicate sensibilities of certain contemporary readers passing into unconsciousness upon tripping over such an object, I may further veil my meaning by referring to that specific part of the male anatomy through the use of *euphemism*, with the employment of such nominals as "gear," "compass," "Johnson," "transcendental signifier," or "woodie," the last intended to contain a clear religious connotation vis-à-vis a reference to the crucifixion. Specifically, by my references to this particular euphemism for the male generative organ, I intend to reference not the London School of Economics but rather the New York Stock Exchange, which like said male member, is apt to rise and fall unexpectedly.

6 Sixth, and last, though of course not least (There is no least in criticism, just as there is no judicious limit to length), since the Word is Flesh, I recommend the reader of this commentary attempt as best as he or she can to approximate their bodily movements to best approximate the tone and import of my words. Perpend: For example, while studying this textual commentary, try as best you can to imitate the facial reaction of a typical viewer of a daytime quiz show or soap opera, or, even better, adjust your facial muscles to imitate those of a steady player of video games such as Call of Duty, ie: eyes blank, mouth dropped open, tongue out, with appropriate salivation, so as to receive the Communion of pixels about to float from the screen down into the mouth, ears, or whatever orifice he chooses to grant entrance to THE TRUTH, with the longing expectation that the boon he is about to receive will enlighten his mind and move his bowels to their best proper function.

I now entrust this commentary into my reader's hands with the humble assertion that it is worthy to be read by every human being born to die. I can only hope that I have done proper homage to the genius that was Ed Schleicher, and if any awards, grants, or fellowships should happen to come my way as a result of the publication of this tome, I can only accept them with the sense of worthiness with which they are offered. I am, after all, no atramentous scribbler of dragon tales with glow-in-the-dark covers, but a widely respected auto-didact, diligent scholar, beloved critic, and karaoke champion of Cheyenne County, Montana.

(1) Linguists and literary historians appear uncertain concerning the question of which, if any, specific "F" word so offended Mr. Schleicher that he felt compelled to censor it as if it spelled out the name of the God of the Old Testament. One commentator, H. Hilarius, suggests that the secret word might be "Frankfurter," since Mr.

Schleicher, who was known to be inordinately fond of this particular form of nourishment, preferred not to be continually reminded of the numerous speculations (many of them most irresponsible) of the possible ingredients in this specific meat source. However, competing exegesisists have uncovered an unverified source that suggests the actual word in question is "Fuckfarter," a possible reference to equally unverified claims that Mr. Schleicher may have been—at times—unfaithful to his wife, and that his excessive consumption of dubious flesh substances may have affected his gastric behaviors. We do know that this word was known to have been used aloud on numerous occasions by one R. Mutt, an ex-Eddite, when Mr. Schleicher rejected his request that the Eddite scripture be amended so as to allow for the burning, not just of books, but of the authors themselves. The most logical speculation remains, as noted by M. Scriblerius (2017), that when pronounced slowly, the word, through Lockean association of ideas, might have reminded Schleicher of his own private suspicions regarding the wisdom of his diet. Another possibility is that this mental association led Schleicher to an irrational fear of committing an anal eructation while he was delivering one of his public sermons. To support this theory, I sight Metzger's little-known theory that religious sermons might have their source in bodily functions. To support his thesis, Metzger quotes Henry Adams: "The kinetic theory of gas is an association of ultimate chaos." Any reference to Metzger, of course, needs to be qualified by the unfortunate fact that he was later arrested for indecent exposure when he attempted to mount a Rodin exhibition in The Hague.

Of course, each of these theories may be true, false, or true and false, depending on denotative and connotative logical reasoning or one's personal use of Venn Diagrams. As the Sybil of Delphi proved, the passing of gasses is never a mere coincidence, but often a sign of divine revelation. Granted, as a strict rationalist I reject out of hand any claims to the truth of revelations other than my own, and associate such behavior with rank superstition. The only true "revelations" in today's modern world are internet "reveals," "easter eggs," and movie "spoilers."

Furthermore, as will be demonstrated later, I am no Devout. Still, to paraphrase Horatio, there are more things in heaven and intestines than are dreamed of in philosophy.

(2) The decease of irony was widely-reported in the press at the time (November, 2016). The word has now been omitted from some dictionaries, and not just by Eddites. One theory traces the trouble to a high school English teacher, Edwina Parse, who included among her assigned readings Johnathan Swift's "A Modest Proposal." Apparently her students misread the piece as being pro-abortion, and as a result, burned the book and then the school. Ms. Parse attempted to redeem herself in court, but before she could, she tragically passed away from terminal anaphora. Before long the mortality rate connected with this word "irony" increased exponentially, until in order to protect their teachers, schools initiated the practice of simply banning the word itself. In fact, some school boards have even gone so far as to replace the word irony in books with the term "literal truth." In fairness to Mr. Schleicher, there is no evidence to suggest that he ever openly supported the immolation of people, let alone teachers.

(3) If the reader will forgive the seeming anomaly of a footnote inside a footnote, the editor wishes to note the added possibility that this tragic event might have been connected in some way to the suggestion made to Schleicher from the aforementioned R. Mutt, and to the added possibility that any practice of immolating teachers might lead to a drain on the education budget. Mr. Mutt reportedly died in 1999 from exfoliation.

**The Devouts**

The second recently discovered scripture is more problematic. It appears to have no name, no founder, no church, no list of commandments or prohibitions, no congregations, no requirements for membership, and indeed, with several debatable exceptions, no membership. They are, rather, a loose and open collection of what

Melville called "Isolatoes," who just happen to have been pulled from the depths by the same net of random wonder. They have no specific doctrine, though elements of Buddhism, Hinduism, Taoism, Spiritualism, Christian mysticism, and the Ramones have been identified as possible influences. The followers of this absurd cult appear to believe that people who rely on social media *are not really communicating*. Therefore, in order to preserve true language, they rely on covert means of communication using only the written word, and in a format that requires such outmoded absurdities as pen, paper, cursive, touch, and scent. Furthermore, some of the more fanatical followers of this cult have had the brazen temerity to assert that frequent fliers in cyberspace exhibit symptoms of paranoid schizophrenia, that they spend countless hours worrying over their image in the eyes of anonymous viewers, constructing a false model or simulacrum of themselves to fool the casual observer, then, like Narcissus (a hero to the Eddites) fall in love with their own creation.

The Devout text has been decoded by this editor and other linguists and literary historians, plus hundreds of investigators on the internet, from numerous and varied sources, including:

1 Original papers of total strangers.

2 Symbols and hieroglyphs found in the designs of some postage stamps, on the tops of city buildings, or spray-painted on the sides of railroad cars.

3 Messages folded and placed inside hollow trees and in cracks in the walls of tenement houses.

4 Wrong-number phone calls.

5 A purported conversation between W.B. Yeats and the ghost of a swan.

6 A man suffering from a seemingly permanent case of hiccoughs.

7 The sound emitted by Mrs. Edwina Killbury when her six year old daughter poked her in the stomach with a huge log.

8 Television commercials played backwards so that the products un-sell themselves.

9 Strange but beautiful music some people claim to be emanating from clouds on certain days. No specific pattern of days has been established. No specific type of cloud pattern has been identified.

10 Strange but beautiful people.

11"Visions" of those searching for these scattered scriptures of strange men shifting movie sets around and by doing so changing their home towns to places they cannot recognize.

12 Words accidentally released from opened library windows.

13 Whispers passed from chessboard to chessboard.

14 The secret dreams of lonely people everywhere as they talk in their sleep.

15 Wind chants heard in the cornfield where Buddy Holly died.

16 Secret messages written on the inside of the Lone Ranger's mask.

17 Footnotes to a number of articles from which they have somehow become detached.

18 The lyrics to a child's song, 1963, as she skipped rope.

19 Selections from a suppressed book by Dr. Ray Gamma, *Everything is Made Up of Tiny Little Things.*

20. Excerpts from a newspaper article concerning the death of Dr. Gamma due to accidental self-irradiation.

21 Scraps and tattered fragments of conversations, nighttime sidewalks small town America, that floated like burning leaves up to the

bedroom windows of children whispering bed to bed, trying to decode the adult world, the world of forever alone.

22 Whatever sparkles, or even emits individual sparks.

23 The silence between drops of rain.

24 A collection of old longings, swept from gutters, pulled from garbage heaps, simply captured in mid-air.

25 The lyrics from the B-side of every one-hit-wonder record.

26 The secret language of birds.

27 Light moving from crow shadow to crow shadow.

28 The Christmas tree lights of childhood, which contained not only light and color, but specific emotions related to them.

29 The last words of a butterfly.

30 Every line of love, forgiveness, or passion ever not spoken by anyone.

The vast majority of the poems contained in this volume were collected by your diligent editor, using as his sources the thirty listed above, and I believe I can assert with all due modesty that I am the world's leading expert on this cult. Granted, I lack any training or university degree in theology, but this is irrelevant since Devoutism is not a religion, plus it will certainly come clear to my readers before finishing their intense study of this exegesis that my frequent stays in motels all over this great nation provide the perfect opportunity to seek out every possible location for the Devouts' hidden missives. This has entailed visiting literally hundreds of different locations, some of them representing dangers and risks of almost unimaginable proportions. Unfortunately, it also led to several arrests for voyeurism that I adamantly deny and am forcefully pursuing through the courts. Suffering is the natural concomitant to greatness.

Nefastis and Maxwell (2022) were perhaps the first to assert that one goal of the Devouts is to communicate in a manner completely outside of the internet, hence outside text-messaging and its factotums, such as Facebook, Twitter, and Tik Tok, with the goal of increasing the energy and originality of ideas and countering the sameness and conformity so typified by the use of Emoji and other entropy-inducing memes. Of course this is only a desperate claim made by the Devouts themselves, who have clearly never tasted the exquisite delights of our best internet poets, many of whose best poems, once having been fixed with a good spellcheck, clearly rank with those of Keats, Shelley, Dickinson, or any other poet in that bible of undergraduates everywhere, *The Norton Anthology of Poets.* The theory purported by Nefastis and Maxwell is certainly possible, and if so, supersedes my own theory (though unlikely), published on my website and repeated on my podcast, that Devouts are simply anti-social creatures possessed with a neurotic need for privacy. They also appear, for some unfathomable reason, to believe in both the possibility of revelation and the sacredness of the written word. This fact might indeed justify naming them a religion, although I suspect a more accurate nametag might be lunacy (for more information, see my comment appearing earlier in this tome, an original observation of my own, on the debate over the diverse possible meanings of gastrointestinal disturbances).

Nevertheless, it remains a possibility, of course, that the only true adherents of this "religion" are the researchers ourselves, of which this editor, in all modesty, stakes a claim on being the most significant and well-known. I realize I have made this claim before, but experience in the Ivory Tower has taught me the vital lesson that a literary critic or editor cannot too often assert his own priority over the interpretations of lesser mortals than himself. However, the outside chance possibility that the "evidence" we have so diligently gathered, collated, indexed, memorized and published online might really amount to nothing more than a random wandering of words and images that form hints and clues only in the creative mind of the reader, must be faced down and, where possible, forcefully refuted or at least tracked to questionable sources, such as libraries. This possibility—that the researchers ourselves have accidentally invented the very reality we are explicating— must be fully explicated and disproven if our current field of critical and textual analysis is to achieve full standing in academia. Contrary to claims made by my enemies, I do not, in fact, begin each investigation with the answer, and then work backwards towards the question. Even the breath of such an assertion constitutes a libel, or a liberal, and I am also pursuing this diligently through the courts. I am committed.

As an example of just how diligent and brave this editor is, I offer the modest boast that I was successful last year in tracking down an actual alleged Devout. After attempting to contact him by mail, phone, and Fed Ex package, circling the house where he allegedly lives numerous times and making careful notations concerning his entrances and exits, tossing pebbles at his windows, pursuing him by car across six state lines and accidentally running him off a highway, I did at last succeed in convincing the subject to agree to an interview.

From his hospital bed, the subject refused to admit that he is, in fact, a Devout, but I took this as no denial, but rather, in fact, as a potential confirmation of my suppositions, given the Devouts' known reluctance to publically expose themselves. Moreover, he conceded that he has heard of the Devouts and has read some of their alleged poetry, which he claims to have snatched from winds blowing around his home town of _________. He further conceded that the refusal by the Devouts to make use of the internet may be short-sighted, though he himself does not have an internet connection. He insists he is no Luddite, but confesses to a mortal fear of Emoji and "Selfies." He was unable—or unwilling—to offer up the names of any of his fellow Devouts. Perhaps he fears a possible blacklist.

I have collected in this volume all the known extant texts of the Devout Movement. This editor concedes that the no Devout poet has yet been known to charge money for his or her work, a sure sign of insanity. However, it should seem clear to any objective reader that this current collection is unprecedented in its scope and ambition. The book, in short, is well worth its price, even if the current price were to climb precipitously in conjunction with my legal costs. This curious—and dare I say un-American—desire among Devouts to avoid a simple and potentially rewarding avenue for profit perhaps contributes to the belief among Eddites (all of whom, so far as I know, have websites and podcasts) that the Devouts constitute a subversive organization, perhaps necessitating a government investigation.

And so, my dear and diligent reader, I present to you two vital examples of modern religious faith, one good, one ill. Each text is fully annotated and explicated by myself, and if I may be granted a rare foray into immodesty, I believe I can honestly assert than in many if not most cases, my annotations and explications are more detailed and accurate than the originals. I modestly propose, also, that at least my reader—as opposed to my numerous detractors—accept the fact that I have come closer than any other literary or historical investigator to penetrating the absolute truth of this phenomena of the Eddites vs. the Devouts, a conflict, if I may be so bold, as memorable as that between the Moderns and the Ancients. I have composed this scripture under pressures that would have broken any mere mortal long ago, pursued by legal authorities and psychiatric lunatics while often composing hurriedly under the dim bulbs in the dire rooms of nameless motels as I flee the Deep State. Dangers lie awaiting me everywhere, and sirens pursue me like haunted cats.

B.S.

# Contents

# The Secret History of the Origin of Everything

—By Edward Schleicher (4)

A brief note from the Bookseller and publisher of The Laputa Press: As previously stated, this is the only known, editorially approved, extant copy of this historical text, copiously documented and annotated, and bound in imitation leather and gold. Therefore, if I may briefly betray an immodesty, well-worth its asking price of $79.99. This scholar is well-aware of the many defamations that have been leveled at this scripture, some even going so far to claim that, like *The Protocols of the Learned Elders of Zion,* it is fact a bigoted and mean-spirited forgery, and no more. This editor vehemently denies these charges, and therefore reiterates the just price of this volume of explication and erudition. In his mind, there is no doubt that Ed Schleicher was in point of fact an historical personage, though whether or not he was a god he leaves up to the reader, of course. However, there can be no denying the fact that Schleicher's scriptures declaring the high holiness of all self-interest have served as an inspiration to his millions of followers, and have even begun to overtake and replace the scriptures of Ayn Rand, for the simple reason that Rand's books are exceedingly long and often betray a disturbingly lurid interest in sex. Therefore, without further delay, the text begins below. One more thing: It is absolutely untrue, despite the claim of the discredited author of *The Real History of Ed,* that Book One of *The Secret History of the Origin of Everything* was written by a fish.

Book One: In the Eddening:

1 In the beginning was the Word, and the Word was with Ed, and the Word was Ed. Thus all humans are rightfully referred to as Eddites, sole possessors of the absolute truth of Ed.

2 And Ed said: "Let the be light," with the help of my new, TOTAL SECURITY EMERGENCY FLASHLIGHT, ONLY $99.99, WITH TAX."

3 Ed invented Adam and Eve, who fell from grace for their disobedience to Ed's Word. (5) They fell from innocence because they trusted the word of The Serpent, a known and practicing liberal.

4 Adam and Eve, (NOT Adam and Steve) were __ruit—ul and multiplied, and they produced a line of powerful male children outshone in strength, daring, and brilliance only by Ed's own two sons, who were godlike, like himself.

5 After Eviction, Adam and Eve collected their deposit and went forth upon the earth to spread the word of Eddism.

6 Mr. and Mrs. Potato Head (6) eventually died from a bug infestation, but luckily for mankind, Ed, at their funeral, provided his devoted flock with the following Commandments:

I Thou shalt not lie, cheat, or steal, unless a reasonable chance of getting away with it appears. Profit is always good, poverty always evil. Therefore, I, the holy Ed, hereby declare that the retirement age be raised to 110.

II Thou shalt have no gods before me. I am the only god named Ed, and that's all there is to it. Contrary to Nietzsche's claim, Ed is not dead. This is fully in line with the line from that famous poet, Horace Mann, who wrote: "O Navis, in mare te tovi, etc.", which, accurately translated, means, "Don't change anything. Vote for Me."

III Jesus was not my son, but one of my prophets. When, dying on the cross, he asked me, "Father, what the heck did I ever do?" (7) he was speaking to me but in a metaphorical, not a literal sense. It is a well-known fact that I am not responsible for anything.

IV Thou shalt not make any graven images of me unless full copyrights for all profits are signed to by legal contract. This includes:

T-shirts, sweaters, socks, jocks, panties, coffee mugs, bumper stickers, posters, banners, flags, fanny-pillows, other kinds of pillows, pistols, rifles, shape-charge bombs, Zippo lighters, or any other sellable object that might contain my sweet and holy image pasted, painted, engraved, or photo-shopped onto it.

V Thou shalt not kill unless really necessary. An Eddite is a committed isolationist, unless the war can be fought far from America's shores and shown in television bites as nighttime entertainment.

VI Thou shalt not commit adultery, unless your wife is a supermodel, in which case she probably won't care.

VII Each night before going to bed, thou shalt repeat these holy words: "May Ed bless himself, for he is truly amazing, incredible, stupendous and a winner like nobody's ever seen before". And may all Ed's enemies (who are also enemies of the people) be cursed as stupid, lazy, horrible, terrible, disgraceful and losers like nobody's ever seen before.

VIII Dear Ed Schleicher:

I hate your stinking fucking creepy-crawling hypocritical guts, you slab of disgusting, pulsating, putrefying SPAM. You are as distinctive as dirt and about as entertaining as watching other people bowl. You fink, you fake, you fuck, you fusty Milk Dud with no caramel, you frankfurter fart on the living room floor, you radioactive roadkill. I want to ask you: Why are your suits always the size of church tower bells? Does David Byrne know you raid his wardrobe? Why does your tie always drag on the ground like the tongue of a pedophile at Disney World? And what's up with your hair? It looks like a comb-over on top of somebody else's comb-over. I'd like to stick your head in a vise and squeeze it till your shaggy eyebrows pop right off. I await your imminent demise with such bated breath that I can barely breathe, you and your disgusting spawn. Your entire doctrine was written by a fish, using a Jewish space laser. Away with you, trumpet of wind, you giddy son of a real estate huckster, you cheeky twit without a twitter, have the courage of your lack of convictions and disappear forever into cyberspace.

Yours in Hellfire,

The Singing Bone (8)

(3.a) The commentator requests the reader's kind indulgence if he asserts here the simple fact that, as the number of my words contained in this document actually exceeds the number of words in Schleicher's book, in some ways I, and not he, may reasonably be considered the true author of this tome. As an example of my modest brilliance, I might note that Ed Schleicher's original Commandments were actually worded as "You Damn Well Better" or "You Damn Well Better Not." I was I, your intrepid guide to this testament, who revised the original version to better approximate the wording of the Old Testament, somewhat in the same manner as the great film director, Cecil B. De Mille, revised that same somewhat dated tome to be in better alignment with modern religious tastes, such as the inclusion of dancing scenes involving much twisting and gyration and cleavage. Any document worn threadbare may be mended and refurbished as needed (See Teufelsdrockh, op. sit, et al., et cetera, ad hominem).

–B.S.

(1) The Nag Yomama author, in his eternal cynicism, amends this text to state: "In the beginning Ed made two Eddites: Mr. and Mrs. Potato Head, whose thick-headedness was inherited by all of their stupid tribe. These two dimwits were tricked by a talking snake into committing unoriginal sin, and as a result the rest of us have to suffer and die. Good one, you two illiterate spuds." I include this vicious parody merely to demonstrate the lurid, naughty, and adolescent tone of this deservedly anonymous scribe, and to show how untrustworthy his

reading of the canonical text of Eddism is in comparison with that of your hard-working editor.

(2) Here our persistent cynic, the purported author of the Nag Yomama text, cannot restrain himself from this sophomoric aside: "Mr. and Mrs. Potato Head begat and begat hundreds of offspring, and Ed insisted on listing every goddamn one of them."

However, in deference to this insidious corrupter of language, this editor concedes that Schleicher may indeed have fostered numerous offspring. In his book he only names two: Don and Eric, whom he also frequently alludes to as "Thing One" and "Thing Two." However, on eighteen occasions that this editor has been able to tally, at his Holy Pep Rallies Schleicher appears to have accidentally blurted out a vague reference to "my eighteen unknown children." It is possible that he was intending to refer to eighteen sermons, but he has apparently made other slips of the tongue, once referring to "The Little Bastards" when he was clearly intending a reference to The Little Rascals. Eddites insist these anomalies merely represent errata or even corruptions of Schleicher's sermons, and that he was in fact referring to "my numerous children of God." This editor, however, stands by the scrupulous accuracy of his research. Moreover, it is more than likely that Schleicher, when he did discuss the admittedly unnerving topic of human reproduction, employed the use of the word "begat" in place of the obscene word, "f____," that he rightfully feared and detested. To this day, an Eddite, when overcome with the temptation to anger, is apt to make use of such terms as "Oh yeah? Well begat you," and "Begat, begat, begat my begatting job."

(6) Clearly, this is an Errata. "Adam and Eve" is correct. This editor suspects that the allusion to toys of the 1950's and 1960's was inserted on the sly by our ubiquitous mocker of holy texts. If so, the joke is at his own expense, since I caught him in the act, ha-ha. It is a simple fact, well-known among theological historians, that Adam and Eve actually died in a Zealot drive-by shooting. Furthermore, I am

myself a passionate consumer of French Fries during my numerous stops at fast-food drive-thru windows, and I am exceedingly unsettled by the blasphemous implication that all this time I might have been unintentionally cannibalizing my religious ancestors. The aforementioned drive-by shooting is not to be confused with THE GREAT NUN SHOOTOUT OF 2023, a mass casualty event, where two groups of nuns arguing over an obscure point of religious doctrine took the will of God into their own hands, with predictable results.

(7) Once again our inveterate practical joker appears to be at work. One would suspect he could content himself with drawing mustaches on copies of the Mona Lisa.

(8) This, too, is clearly an errata, or erratum, depending on your use of classical Latin, perhaps inserted by the author of the dubious volume supposedly found at the questionable Nag Yomama. In fact, it is just possible that the prankster himself is the face behind the moniker of "The Singing Bone." Either way, this nomenclature alone is an insult to German fairy tales, which are well-known for their delightful take on nature and human nature, so much so that they have even been credited by some literary historians as serving as a possible inspiration to Adolf Hitler, who was famous for his enthusiastic consumption of fairy tales.

The correct Eighth Commandment of Ed reads:

"Sensitivity is weakness, indifference is strength, love is hate, privacy is obscenity, difference is chaos, uniformity is coherence, conformity is faith, insurrection is tourism."

The reader can plainly see the much higher level of ethics, morality, and intellectual acumen reflected in the actual scripture, versus the adolescent obscenities voiced by our childish scribbler of counter-narratives.

IX: Thou shalt covet everything that is not nailed down except thy neighbor's ass. However, thou may covet thy neighbor's wife's ass providing thou doesest thy coveting in private. Also, thou shalt not nail thy ass to the ground, as then thou will not be able to attend my rallies.

X From this moment forward, all followers of the Eddite faith will forswear forever all uses of the fully frivolous letter "F" when fronting a word. Furthermore, the faithful are forever forbidden from frequent use of the following utterances: "F… you," "Oh, f…did I leave the oven on?" "F….. up," "Go f…yourself," F…a duck," "F…….e," "f…dom, and "Hey, you wanna f…?" Violators of this commandment will either be excommunicated or forced to move to Akron.

XI This is not an extra commandment, since as God Ed I can add as many commandments as I damn well please. This Commandment covers anything I met have left out of the other Commandments. For God's sake, think for yourself. Or just make something up.

XII Even though the first eleven commandments printed here clearly cover any and all possible human truths, good old Ed is adding this extra one just in case. Please feel free to include any commandment you wish here, so long as it does in no way violate THE ABSOLUTE TRUTH of my previous commandments. Any violation, intended or no, may incur my wrath and force me to take an aspirin. Signed: Your Lord, Ed.

Addendum: Mine is The Voice in the Wilderness! Mine is the Call to Rebirth! Be no longer a Chaos, America! From now on be only a Schleicher!

Dear Lord Ed:

I was thrilled to itching to see that you took the advice I gave you in the six hundred and sixty-six letters I have recently sent to you. I realize that I violated your law against communication in any form other than text message by doing so, but I just couldn't help myself. I had to find some way of conveying to you my theory that any list of commandments should equal twelve commands, nor more, nor less. This is to make sure that your list mirrors the number 12 as it appears in the Holy Bible, the second-most important book in the world, next to your own. Some examples include: The twelve tribes of Israel, the twelve stages of the Zodiac, the Zodiac Killer, the twelve apostles of Jesus, and my own particular favorite, "A baker's dozen." As you know, Jesus was particularly fond of bread, so I suggest you include at least one baker as one of your apostles. Without sounding proud, I believe that I would be an excellent choice for this roll, I mean, role.

Sincerely,

Anita Dickenme

PS: I am the one who collects all the sweat off your discarded handkerchiefs at your public sermons and "Ah ha!" rallies in order to bottle and sell my own brand of holy water, which has proven quite lucrative, so thank you again.

PS redux: I might also take this opportunity, if I may be so bold, to warn you against the blasphemous claims against you made by a certified lunatic who calls himself Dr. Botkin Shade. I recommend he be condemned to a life in Akron ASAP (9).

(9) At this point, my patience is at an end. This is one of the most egregious of all libels that has ever been levied against your sinless editor and exigesisist. I am not now, nor have I ever been, "a certified lunatic." While it is certainly true that I have made several rest stays in certain sanatoriums around this great nation, I have always proved successful within the 72 hour hold limit of using my amazing language powers and rhetorical gifts to argue my way to freedom by convincing all—and I stress all—of my psychiatrists that they were wrong and I was right. And I gently request the reader not forget that it was I who, in a justly famous monograph, thoroughly disproved Freud's Oedipus Complex theory by showing that, in point of fact, young boys do not desire to sexually possess their mothers, but rather their first cousin, twice-removed.

Furthermore, I venture the claim here that clearly there IS no such person as Anita Dickenme, and, in fact, this entire missive is yet another attempt by the Fleet Street reject and author of the Nag Yomama disproven text to mock the nobility of all my research. Some internet wags have taken such license with the truth as to assert that I am, myself, the real Anita Dickenme, and that Dr. Botkin Shade is a mere invention of an internet prankster, or even—a shudderingly base gossiping—that I am both Botkin and Anita, and that I am currently employing the internet name of "Bonita." These are such obvious cases of post hoc fallacious reasoning, that I will simply leave it to the kind faith of my devoted reader to ferret out the truth, which, I suggest, like Ms. Dickenme, is staring him directly in the face. I have never known a Dickenme, and if I did find one sitting in my family tree, I would most certainly toss it in the nearest waste paper basket. —Ed (Editor) (Angry)

PS: As proof of my assertion above, I am including below a brief excerpt from the Nag Yomama manuscript, so that the discerning reader may identify the clear similarity in tone and word choice between this document and the letter from Ms. Dickenme. Clearly, the same naughty, sinister author penned both in a cruel effort to question this editor's authority.

One further note: If the reader does not mind my assuming an assumption, I want to reassure his likely belief that literary critics and editors, and not poets, are the unacknowledged legislators of mankind. This assertion, as it were, I hope will not strike my gentle reader as an assertion of unearned pride, notwithstanding the infamous attack on my profession made by that mad satirist, Jonathan Swift, when he penned these spiteful words: "A malignant deity, called Criticism [that] dwelt on top of a snowy mountain in Nova Zembla." This quote may well have applied to the Dunciad denizens of the Age of Enlightenment, but as is commonly conceded, nowadays, in our current Age of Entertainment, the science of criticism has evolved to such a degree that, if I my so assert, we seem to be rapidly approaching a time when poetry and history may be discarded altogether and replaced with literary critics and book editors—B.S.

"How The World Really Began—a Counter-Ed scripture unearthed at Nag Yomama

The world is really a giant egg laid by Ed one morning when he believed he was suffering from a mere case of Ball Park wieners stomach cramps, until he suddenly laid an egg, and just as suddenly remembered that he had partied hardy the night before, gotten blasto-drunk, and fucked a swan. This swan later served as his queen and they had many boy and girl swans between them. Later claims that Ed himself later grew webbed feet remain unproven.

Ed ruled as king of the world but was too drunk to write down any commandments. Ed did claim at one point that a Paraclete swan descended from heaven, laid an egg on his head, and when the egg hatched, it contained The Gospel According to Ed. This, of course, is sheer nonsense. Ed never did anything but chase women and steal children's breakfast cereal. The swan did all the ruling.

The swan also invented baseball, even thinking so far ahead as to place giraffes around the outside of the playing field fence to catch home run balls. Meanwhile, Ed made six attempts at walking on water, all of them unsuccessful.

Ed had two sons, Don and Eric. Don was torn from the thigh of a chicken, and Eric was declared the world's first and only prenatal lobotomy."

Note from B.S., your noble editor and critic:

I believe by now the reader can see there is no point in going on with this madness, so let us return to *The Secret History of the Origin of Everything*, specifically to that portion of the book that correlates to our own New Testament:

*The Secret History of the Origin of Everything*, continued: The

Sherman on the Mount

And so Ed ventured forth from Akron to spread the word of Ed. Soon he had collected twelve Apostles. Their names were: Trotha, Putz, Judaintus, Ficken, Todd, Paduk, Samizdat, Wakefield,

Nostril, Pinguid, Blitzen, and Scheissbug. (10)

Ed led his flock a mission to spread the Truth of his Word throughout the American South. Near the sunken nation of Atlantis, he mounted a great hill of Confederate Christmas calendars and spoke to all the Sherman on the Mount (11)

The Sherman:

—Blessed are the rich, for they are the makers of wealth, some of which will trickle slowly down to the poor.

—Woe to the poor, for they are lazy, and in punishment for their sloth, all educational opportunities are to be denied them.

—Blessed is the Defense Department, for protecting us from all the other nations who love us.

—Blessed are chokeholds, for they protect us from the homeless.

—Love your neighbor as yourself, unless your neighbor is Black, Native American, Mexican, Costa Rican, Honduran, Vietnamese, Chinese, Ukrainian, Canadian, Jew, Muslim, Hindu, Buddhist, Catholic, agnostic, atheist, existentialist, artist, teacher, author, professor, journalist, chess enthusiast, liberal, gay, bi, trans or uncertain, poor, drag queen, impoverished drag queen, psychologist, poet, social justice advocate, social worker, civil rights advocate, voting rights advocate, supporter of free speech, believer in separation of church and state, watcher of French films, eater of French fries, avant-garde, fan of rock and roll, fan of rap, fan of fun, individualist, anti-consumerist, or cloud-watcher.

In any of these cases, you may declare this person to be un-American, burn down their house, and drive them out of your town. You may also send them mean messages on Twitter, complete with mocking Emoji.

—Austerity is prosperity. We must turn back the clock on America to the wonderful 1930's, a time when the correct people prospered, family values flourished, and people were content with what they had. Dorothy Gale's dust farm, rightly-seen, is the ideal homestead. (12)

(10) Of these Apostles, the most famous is probably Ficken, who thrice-denied Ed's demand for free season tickets to the national skeet shoot, and was punished for his sin by toppling from the top tier of a tractor-pull and being crucified upside down in the popcorn concession stand. Ficken is also a kind of Judas figure in the Ed scripture, since his first name began with the letter "F." In terms of the Eddite ideology, this fact perhaps rendered him morally suspect from the first.

(11) I have searched diligently on Google Maps for the lost nation of Atlantis, but alas to no avail. By my best historical estimates, Ed actually led his ever-growing flock to a landfill outside Atlanta dedicated to General Edward, "Wrongway" Hunley, who famously, or infamously, attacked his own army at the little-known Second Battle of Atlanta. Apparently, Hunley was attempting a rear-guard action against General Sherman when he led a night-time march that somehow managed to circle the entire Confederate army instead. As a result, in the morning he stormed General Lee in the rear, the first and only known time that such a thing had ever happened to General Lee.

(12) Regrettably, here your faithful editor must bring this important text to an end. As it is, I have been forced by expediency and the injustice forever inflicted upon creative artists by a repressive society to type much of this document while moving from rancid hotel to rancid hotel as I trek across the country. (I never knew there even WAS a "No-Tell Motel," at least it is the only motel where I have stayed to rest and compose whose name I can precisely identify). The reader is assured

that most of what I excluded from this narrative was so badly burned or so assiduously censored as to be virtually unreadable.

I must now, with joy pressed forever to my lips, depart. It appears that the supposed Devout whom I so most accidentally drove off a state highway has decided to press charges against me for reckless endangerment and attempted kidnapping, so I must be on my way. Art is long but the law is longer.

B.S.

# The Book of the Devout

Publisher/Bookseller's note to the reader: As you can see, the eminent Professor Botkin Shade was unable to finish his work on this manuscript, though for some reason he appears to have believed he had done so. Since his current whereabouts are unknown, I have taken upon myself the heavy mantle of completing his commentary. In lieu of this responsibility, I wish to offer the following notifications:

It is the humble opinion of this editor that even though the manuscript you hold in your generous hands is unfinished, it is nevertheless a complete and valuable work of erudite scholarship. Thus sayeth I, the editor of this editor. In support of my claim, I may in all modesty note that other works of this same revered scholar, Professor Botkin Shade, are available from the Laputa Press, among them:

The Absolute Truth of Relativism

Austerity: Un-Christian or Just Good Sense?

An Explanation of Explanations

The Assassination of President Lincoln: A Musical in Two and a Half Acts

A Thorough Exegesis and Etymology/Ontology of the Letter F, with Maps and Concordance

How to Achieve Peace and Serenity by Contacting Your Inner Clam

How to Fart in Seven Languages (currently out of stock)

*How to Cheat at Chess*

Each of these works of scholarship published by this press, I might add, is available on the Laputa Press for prices that vary with our

"Butterfly Ballot" method of pricing our products. The only one of these masterpieces concerning which I hold any reservations is *How to Cheat at Chess*. Chess, as any aspiring grandmaster such as myself knows, is a game of logic, memory, and skill, and it appears that the only cheating strategy that Professor Botkin suggests for game use in his book is to attach a mirror to the top of your head to distract your opponent and have a partner stand behind your opponent to send you secret hand signals advising you on your next move. As for the book dealing with intestinal eructates, it is clearly not on the list of masterpieces available from this Bookseller, and I only include it here as evidence that Professor Botkin and myself are indeed, often in complete agreement, despite the claims of our many envious detractors and enemies. Botkins asserted, and I agree, that the book named above was yet another vicious parody penned by the naughty anti-wordsmith author who so plagued the good Botkin that the latter, poor man, was driven to standing on his head and whistling popular tunes day and night.

As the devoted reader is no doubt aware, the admirable Dr. Botkin is also the pen behind no fewer than nine thousand seven and hundred and forty-three monographs, including the uniquely memorable

*How To Be Your Own Lover*, but these indispensable tomes are easily available on the internet on the primary websites dedicated to the study of the wisdom of the divine Ed. Moreover, six of Botkin's most highly praised (with smile emoji) articles will soon be published on my Laputa Press website, thanks to the diligent efforts of the late Dr. Thomas Tubtale, who was tragically removed from our mortal midst at the tender age of fifty-seven after being nibbled to death by a herd of tame geese, otherwise known as "Critics." Dr. Tubtale, as has been reported in numerous websites, was the first and only graduate of Wikipedia University.

Due to Professor Boktins' untimely departure from the scene, the responsibility for collating the following poems has fallen upon me. I do not shrink from this responsibility, I embrace it, and this in the teeth of the fact that I may not know what I am doing. This concession having been made, nevertheless I have assumed my editorial duties with pluck and aplomb. The careful reader will notice my own footnotes that accompany this text, but at this point it may help if I state a few of my operating assumptions concerning the poems in this text:

First, since my footnotes may at times disagree with or even contradict those of Botkin Shade, and since Botkin Shade's current whereabouts are unknown, the reader may assume that whenever such a lacuna in viewpoints occurs, my own reading should take precedence over if not outright replace that of the well-meaning but at times somewhat befuddled professor. I am now the sole possessor of this manuscript, and possession is nine-tenths of the law, and ten tenths of the profits.

Second, I wish to squelch, smother, and break to smithereens a vicious rumor currently circulating online—probably originating with a devious Devout—that I and Professor Botkin Shade are in reality the same person. This absurd theory argues that the good Doctor Botkins' admitted confusion over just how many Botkin Shades there may actually be, and whether he might be one of these Botkin Shades and thus has been unintentionally following himself around the country for some time, that one can extrapolate from this possibility that Dr. Botkin Shade is, so to speak, a paranoid schizophrenic, in other words—to use a somewhat crude colloquialism, a dog chasing its own tail—or tale (cf: Note "A" below concerning Cloudcuck, Montana). I deny this obscene anti-critic conspiracy on two grounds: First, in order for a conspiracy to exist, there must be at least two people involved in the conspiracy, since the very etymology of this word traces to a Latin root meaning "Breathe Together," and since I myself am clearly not breathing together, except when I am blowing up balloons for the under-fives, I am forever breathing alone. Second, I can prove my identity at any time simply by stating my Yahoo password, something I of course refuse to do for the simple reason that an online prankster might steal it and then use it to claim that he is actually myself. Also, I would like to reassure the reader that I always check my reflection in the mirror at least thirty times a day, just to make certain that I still exist, and furthermore, whenever I go out to dinner, I always arrive promptly in time to greet myself when I arrive to partake of my repast. I am also currently working on a series of Selfies which I intend to release on the internet as soon as I can unravel the mystery of which side of my phone is the camera.

Third, based on conversations I held with the good Professor Botkin, plus an assiduous review of his copious notes, I fear I must disagree with his claim that it is possible that one poet composed all of the poems in this particular "scripture." Such a feat would require that our anonymous poet also be almost superhumanly peripatetic, if not downright ubiquitous, not to mention most likely out of his mind. It is far more logical to assume that most of these poems were written by numerous people, rather than subscribe to an interpretation that would argue that one poet was composing one poem at a time, and then secreting them across the country in various obscure locations in order to lead the poor professor on a paranoid wild goose chase (apologies here to Dr. Tubtale). I say this, of course, knowing full well that Professor Botkin appears to have composed much of his own work while subsisting in a seemingly endless number of seamy motels from state to state, and thus qualifies as something of a peripateticition himself. One waggish cynic, who dubs himself "The Singing Bone," has gone so far as to suggest that my good friend Botkin is legally insane, and has in fact composed all these "Devout" poems himself, deposited them in thousands of secret cubbyholes around this great nation, and then suffered complete amnesia concerning everything he has done, thus providing a convenient excuse to review and praise his own work.

Do these poetic anonymousati know one another? It is certainly possible, yet it seems equally possible that they are merely a random collection of lonely people who all feel a need to express a longing for some lost community, some means of communication outside the now commonly accepted (and perfectly normal) one of social media. They are, in short, contemporary Luddites who probably also believe that the earth is flat and that the presidential election of 2020 was not stolen.

It is certainly feasible, of course, that the poems dealing with Donald Trump may have been written by one person. Why this particular poet chose to focus his somewhat childish ire on the well-meaning Mr. Trump, while leaving the more controversial figure of Mr. Biden alone, is not at all clear. However, I see insufficient evidence to conclude with Professor Botkin's speculation that Schleicher and Trump might be the same person in disguise, especially given the apparent evidence of Mr. Schleicher's having committed himself to smoke. Nor can I frankly place much credence in Professor Botkin's speculation that ALL the poems in this volume are really about him. At the risk of offending the sensibilities of an invisible man, I doubt that even a person of Dr. Botkins' well-known erudition would inspire random groups of people to compose poems in his honor. This claim is, in fact, the only one of Professor Botkin's that strikes me as irrational, given the simple fact that, until he disappeared into thin air, the good doctor was not known for violating the laws of reason.

No, it appears to me that Botkins' initial supposition is closer to truth. These poems appear to have been written by a number of different authors who appear to share in common an admittedly irrational and perhaps delusional belief that human communication and belief in something higher than the selfish ego are indispensable qualities for remaining human. There is no accounting for the eccentricities of some people, but the fact that these poets choose to remain anonymous, and their curious way of spreading their poems among the public, are in fact compatible with a speculation that they fear that a growing power of censorship in America is a threat to our very humanity. That this is clearly an egregious hyperbolic overreaction to contemporary political and social realities does not mean that these poets, however alarmist, do not honestly believe in their fears. However, to assert just one example of this odd alarmism concerning censorship, I will offer the simple observation that in all

In all our delicious publishing history, the Laputa Press has never censored one word, not even words beginning with the letter "F." In my case in particular, I have always supported the free use of "f" words, and plan to continue doing so in the future.

Ronald Sanctus Rich

Publisher, The Laputa Press

New Editor of *The Secret History of the Origin of Everything*

All profits to accrue to the New Editor

# The Book of the Devout

## By Anonymous

# The code

A starling balances on a maple tree withe,
inscribing the winds with song.
A grasshopper leaps to my wrist,
her baby clinging to her back.
Suddenly my sadness frees.

Can such moments redeem this time
of alienations? This sad house
spun from the virtual Word?
You may call my words destination gravity.
Pathic language from earth and stars:
So go to work each day.
Be good. Follow their rules,
recite your lines, play the part,
and by all means, wear your disguise.
Then come here when you are alone.

## Come can you see me invisible

Come can you see me invisible,
and are you invisible too?
Can you hide between the boldest lies,
brave a breathless and disappear,
or hover between the question and the answer
where beauty lives?

Can you fade into another's eyes,
and not be seen for days?
Or plant your silence in the sky
and wait for words to rain?
Or delirium your way in winds
to wing and moon and star?

Kaleidoscope your mind in sunlight,
embracing, unfinished, free,
and leave all schools that teach you blind?
Be no more swallowed in alone.
Learn to shimmer into midnight.
Seek heaven bone by bone.

# Conversation with the night

Incandescent ailanthus in the moon,
its tortured branches longing for the gone,
the winds calling for breaths,
and the leaf's prayer
that nothing be lost again.

At dawn the grass comes speaking green,
but now is nearly silent, as the crickets
state their terms of ecstasy and death.
And if I open this old dark stone
will it speak light or a word I'm terrified to hear?
Grace is hypothetical,
and Hell is earth in God's despite.
A kingfisher sings the blues
as my heart beats in rhythm with the stars.
And yet we remain alone.

## Such Magic

Just off U.S. Route 30,
past Mansfield Penitentiary
and The Noah's Ark Museum,
houses turn magically to trailers,
gardens to crippled back yards,
and cars to weary mounds of rust.
It's a rare magic.

A back road hobbles round a bend.
Follow it, you audience volunteer,
keep turning, turning,
past incantations in the weeds,
under a dove-pale moon
and the exitless stars.
What magician guides you down this mystery?

Here you may find me behind the show,
the wizard's helper smoking on his break.
Have a look around, is this real or dream,
a graveyard filled with cars instead of bodies!

Note how the rust in this farm truck
has disappeared most of the front door.
The steering wheel of this wrecked Ford
is slammed straight through the engine,
the windshield gone, driver nowhere to be seen.
My personal favorite — the gutted school bus
with poison oak peering from each window.

A prestidigitator might say: "Well at least it's invisible.
Barbed wire asterisks yield no clues."
But I say: Such magic is required training
to hide the poor inside this land of riches.

# The Christians of Crestline

hammered a wooden cross
on a nervous bend in the road
to mark where a dazed midnight driver
lost his concentration and his life. They
erected a black billboard, and in red:
SIN KILLS. The strip club/bar winked
at them, while across the road
an ostrich watched in wonder.

Night gathers with the strength of drowning waves.
Inside girls are writhing on their poles.
They are locals. They work part-time jobs.
Outside plumes the ostrich farm. Truck drivers
push their hard-earned bills in panties,
and hide their deepest yearnings from their wives.

The ostrich stares at the WELCOME sign:
Girls Wanted: Inquire Within.
Neon tits with a smile below.
The Sheriff squats in the far dead-drunk,
writing a note to all that's unseen,
punctuated with kindness of despair.
We are outside the county lines.

The ostrich tilts her head
to stare at the forgotten stars.
A wind blows down the wooden cross.
The Christians of Crestview sleep in lonely beds
while the ostrich cries in the lovesick air.

# The cathode illumination

Every full moon our television went dark,
its red cathode tube no longer beating,
and all the lights in town went out,
and people died, and others disappeared.

Enter old man Kaski, with his long white beard,
and his magic box, filled with glowing replicas.
The tv lit to life, blood light filled the room,
and people returned to life, and how they loved!

Kaski died, and the television said:
"A purple cloud may come, and it may glow.
Pay no attention, go back to sleep,
all is as safe as supposed to be."

But monsters stepped from the screen in pain,
First Frankenstein, who drowned my brother in his bath,
Mr. Hyde crouched in every corner, bats whirled,
and the Phantom stalked me down the basement stairs.

When my father went missing, half the town vanished.
I watched whole houses carted away like movie sets.
People faded like bad reception, and then just disappeared.
replaced with replicas that only stared and stared.

Yet in a hundred secret places around the town
I found a hidden cathode beating near.
Pulsing, flashing, longing to say,
sending its blood-light through the air.

One whispered: "Don't be afraid.
"This world is a projection, it isn't real.
They cannot win. Seek the cathodes everywhere.
If They blot out the sun, listen to the moon."

## For my father, ditched

One day all the cats and turtles
abandoned
joined their quadruped forces
to track down once for all
their truant owners,
beneath an alien moon.

Where begin?
This world be wild and wildered,
true to nothing, built for sly escapes…
The turtle, a Tiffany lamp
with feet, searches the moon—
half-closed eye of a black cat

pressing claw-cold paws
through a graveyard
deserted, desolate,
left forever in the past,
the moon alone in darkness
drowning in teared reflections.

No new owner will suffice
to fill the heart's pure hole
remains here bleeding time
knowing this world is lost as well
in forever longing,
moonless as a blood eclipse.

# Father silence

You kept you secret pact with silence,
devoured your shadow deep in night,
taught whispers whisper to themselves.

You swallowed all your words and wounds.
The words turned to bats and then to darkness.
The wounds took residence in your eyes.

Scrawled your life's blood in the plaster walls.
I tried and tried to read, but the plaster
broke and scattered in my palms.

You searched letters in your mailbox
with no return addresses,
penned by a hand you never knew.

You sawed and nailed to a terrible whole
something in the basement you kept locked there.
Was it your longed for sunless wings?

How can I sing your silent song?
It feel it floating, crow to distant crow.
A mystery without an ending.

Let my pen turn ventriloquist
to speak as well I can your all alone.
May every poem bring you full to life.

## My father warred his every way

My father warred his every way with time
to build something where all made sense.
He built me an Alamo from solid pine
without a Davy Crockett, so someone
could come out alive from a trail of tears.
And still I cried in fear of death each night.

I was the hidden boy, seeking sanctuary.
I hide between the silence and the dark.
But when my mother's father died, my uncle
said: "There isn't any God," then taught me
how to whistle through a yew leaf. Mother said:
"Don't wave. Don't wave to Grandmother."

My father build a dungeon for my monsters—
Frankenstein, Dracula, the Wolf Man and Creature—
But they escaped into my bedroom closet,
warning of dire things to come. When
my father's mother died, with a communion
wafer in her mouth, he skipped the funeral.
"She beat me," he said, and I drowned in his tears.

My father built a maze for my pet mice.
But no one could find the way out.
The mice went mad, and one mouse ate the other.
When the president was murdered,
they gave us the day off, witches tittered in trees,
and I bounced on my bed for days and days.

My father would have built me my own private world,
a castle reaching from moon to stars,
but everything turned broken and done.
My father ate late at night alone, pondering
dreams, but in his darkening all alone,
He didn't know I was gone so long ago.

## My father's monologue

What are you looking at listen to me.
Did I ever tell you about how my old man
abandoned me when I was just six years old
it was the Depression and he said he couldn't afford
two kids so he was taking my sister with him
so goodbye he patted me on the head and said
be good to your mother Pete my name was Ken
then he left and the last I ever saw of him was
dust kicked up from his receding wheels he said
a family is just a burden he can't afford and
that was it well that was not it we moved
to a tenement house in Chicago
and my mother was an invalid so
I had to support her and both my cousins
age fourteen I was out in the streets
shining shoes and selling newspapers
and missing school and giving all my money
to my mother so she could buy Christmas presents
for my cousins one year all I got was an orange
I ate it whole, skin, seeds and all
and at night you could hear the rats in the walls
gnawing at the wires gnawing at the wood
trying to get in and eat your face off
while you slept and my goddamn mother
grabbed me by the penis in the bath
and said one day this will get you in trouble
and she died years later with a Communion wafer
in her mouth though she used to beat me
with a ruler I resented it she never had one word

of love or encouragement but I know the old man
sent her some money and sometimes rotten fruit
from towns so small the graveyard cried to get out
always with no return addresses the bastard
I hope he starved the nuns beat me too
for bad handwriting and I memorized
whole prayers in Latin I never understood
but I say them in my sleep to this day are you
listening I know you can hear them when
you're trying to sleep at night in the good
warm bed I provided you I gave you
all the things I never had I gave you
this house, food on the table good food
not scraps not rotten fruit and you got
toys at Christmas don't say you don't I
used to stare at the Sears Roebuck catalogue
Christmas issue all December closing my eyes
and imagining the toys I wanted in my mind
until they became so real I could touch them
though I knew I'd never make it alive to
eighteen because those rats came each night
like they were dancing in the walls waiting
for their chance and cockroaches would
drop down from the ceiling into your oatmeal
or crawl up out of the drains cockroaches
the size of a pocket watch and that meant
you were poor the nuns said and that meant
you were dirty and had dirty thoughts and
God was punishing you for your sins so
they'd beat you again and again and the
priest with his filthy hands would make you
say a million Hail Marys as if that ever did
one damn thing to stop the rats and the

cockroaches from crawling inside your dreams
to set up shop there. So that's why I built this house
don't say you helped you handed nails that's all,
Pete, you're nothing, kids are just a burden that's all
and why the hell does your brother never write or call
all he ever did was exercise in the basement and I know
don't tell me he worked hard on this house he worked
hard on this house but it's my house not yours you're just
boarders here sucking my life's blood and now he's starving
himself to death in a trailer somewhere in the middle
of nowhere and you mother left too they all leave, all,
did I tell you about the time that time in Hell
my father left us he called my mother that
damned bitch but he said take care of her
Pete and then he gave us all the air except for
my sister he took her with him and I never
saw her again he patted me on the head and
called me Pete my name is Ken, Ken goddamnit
Ken you hear me he didn't even know my name
even the damn hellish nuns knew my name
they yelled it out at attendance each day
Ken the kid who had no dad I hated them I
hated him too why didn't he take me with him
I hated my mother the bitch she beat me
with a ruler I resented it why didn't he take me
with him I loved him I wanted to be with him
I used to write him letters and dropped them
in mailboxes hoping one find its way to him
and he'd come back the bastard the complete
bastard the nuns knew the kids knew everybody
knew I was the kid with no dad goddamn them
a lot of them died from the flu and a lot of them
died in France or in the Pacific or other places

I dreamed about but never got to we moved here
to Lima when I was twelve and we got evicted
seven times in three years I used to come home from
Saint Rose and see all our belongings pitched out
in the street everything even the toys I could finally
afford with my weekend job at the factory and
the goddamn police were always there helping
the landlord dump our stuff by the curb
for the garbage men to take the garbage men and
I'd curse those cops for taking all our furniture out
and keeping some for themselves but they
just laughed and told me to move goddamn along
alone I was alone my cousins had government jobs
now and lived in an apartment with rats and cockroaches
so I couldn't move there and the nuns here must
have been imported from Chicago cause they still
beat me and made me memorize prayers I never
understood and told me I was going to Hell with
my father if I didn't shape up and make more
money for my mother and stop cursing out
the cops who were only doing their jobs my
goddamn mother did I ever tell you she grabbed
my penis in the bath and said I was headed
for trouble someday if I didn't cut that damn thing
off right now and save everyone a lot of trouble but
she couldn't beat me anymore I was six feet tall
by then and tried out for basketball but my mother
made me quit saying I was too skinny all the kids would
laugh at me I should be working more anyway as
if she ever held a goddamn job her whole worthless
life the bitch she died with a Communion wafer in
her mouth but I skipped the funeral and walked
around and around St. Rose laughing and crying

I hated the nuns and damn if the priest didn't have
filthy hands too and called on Satan to come get
them all and I hated that church but I just kept walking
around it and I still say prayers in Latin in my sleep
you can hear me I know you can saying the words over
and over in perfect memory I was smart but I never
got to go to college you'll go to college though I
gave you everything I never had boy, everything
I never had you owe me but kids are a burden
my old man was right there the old bastard I hope
I meet him on the street someday I'll walk right up
to him, shake his hand, touch his shoulder then
punch the son-of-a-bitch right in the mouth and
look how clean this house is I built it up brick by
brick, panel by panel, put in walls and more walls
and I know you handed every nail in this place
but those things don't matter what does matter is
if I ever spot a rat or a cockroach in this place I'm
gonna blow its fucking head off with a goddamn
bazooka and what was with you why did you when
that time you threw yourself off the house what
was that supposed to prove you missed the stones
below then right you even fucked that up kids are
burdens they'll drive you to the poorhouse did I tell
you my mother died with a Communion wafer in her
mouth and I skipped her fucking funeral and all those
people sent sympathy cards grieving for you in your
heartfelt loss oh God, heartfelt, heart-felt, what did
they know about heart-felt what did they know about
me what does anybody know about anybody,
and some day I'm gonna jump in my car and go tearing
away in a dust cloud just like my old man don't think

I won't I'll turn into the bastard myself just to spite
the whole lot of you why are you just sitting there
why do you look at me like that what are you not saying.
Speak. Say something. Speak.

## The Christmas present

Third grade Christmas party, each kid
brings one gift, huge boxes blushing with bows
except one, wrapped in brown paper,
from the poorest girl in class.
Mine.

I thank her. She is so glad
she cries, and touches my hand.
I seethe inside with envy
for what should have been mine,
all those helicopters, fire trucks, robots…

Mine is a mere sketch pad,
with plastic pen and etcher
transparency, five cents
in any bargain bin
in any dime store in town.

I draw the classroom, pull back
the transparency and step through a window
high above clouds and the blue within blue
to worlds that ripen to gold and silver.

This was her gift to me, never to be lost.
Drawn and erased, drawn and erased,
and yet the traces forever remain.
And still I draw her world close,
and escape it with a wave of my hand,
when tears and ingratitude draw too near.

# The uniform

My brother and I bought our Yankee caps
with our allowance, nineteen-sixty-three.
He in joy, I in despair.
I hated the blue, so dark and sincere.

We stopped at the Pizza Planet,
where the cook chased us out into North Street
with a pizza cutter, cursing and screaming:
"THE SOUTH WILL RISE AGAIN!"

I was six. Did not know what a "Yankee" was,
or what "Confederate" meant,
had never been south of Columbus
or heard of Appomattox.

I only knew I loved the rebel grey.
To me it was all beauty, its smoky shade,
and flag of mysterious meanings.
A pure rebellion against the world.

I imagined my general's uniform
until it turned real, triumphing
over that blue of all evil. I dreamed
my countless victories in the sun.

Never heard the shot that killed me.
Some blue marksman hidden in the sky.
I watched a rose unfold from my heart,
turning my grey to red.

I fell to green and growing,
laughing and crying at once.
Just another boy lost in time,
never to regain his secret world.

## Charlottesville

Fever hangs in the willows.
The man with the cocksure eye
awaits you down this road.
Trees spell their leaves in syllables of fear.
A black ghost and a white ghost
dance a mystery through your past.
Read these August birds, crossed in winds.
A death may carve you mystic,
or leave you chanting in the dust.

The kid with an engine for a heart
has one dream alone,
to give misery its own last name.
The man with the cocksure eye
was General Someone once,
but something's buried beneath his marble.
Beware his phantom statue,
as it cries for the corpse of Honor,
and sinks into the silence of the swamp.

And beware this grieving yesteryear.
Its land lies purge-less in its blood,
and its dead walk torch-lit in the night.

# Make America Great Again

The house is a shrug with cataract windows.
A wall surrounds it, broken with fears.
Out back there's someone in a cage.
There's an attic where a scream abides,
a grandfather clock chock full of secrets.

A mob is coming up the road.
Father Shotgun's in his rocker.
Aunt Shivers glares her hypodermic eyes
at mourners she sees hiding in the mirror.
Rusted through, the stoveheart of this house.
The television glows in cancer blue
the floorboards spreading red a stain.
The mother, pock-marked in hate,
sings Amazing Grace so she won't faint.

Outside, torches chant the night.
The Deputy descends to the cellar,
his flashlight a halo in Hell.
The time has come, there's no escape…
There's someone in the doorway taking notes.

# Qanon

A murderous nostalgia haunts our days,
longing for a past
that never was or could be,
a sentimental cruelty
seeking a cartoon enemy,
and a savior, however undeserving.

These heartless quids from cyberspace
loathe and fear materialism, secularism,
lack of true faith, and all the exiled,
never seeing they are staring in a mirror.

Ideas as coherent as seaweed,
they snatch at the air for conspiracies,
calling for an Auto de Fey, demanding
miracle, mystery and authority
to fill the drilling hole in their hearts.

This will not, cannot end well.
I fear before this ignorant storm abates
Juno's paycock may long to cry again,
frenzy bewilder the mob to vengeance,
the honey bee die in the house of the stare.

## Burn your emoji in Hell

The poem comes together or I fall apart.
So burn your emoji in Hell you're not helping.
Your tweets and texts fall from a dictionary
with barely thirty words, trying and failing
to light the surrounds with their pale fire.

Unused words are blowing in the wind:
crisp verbs, nouns sobbing for the real,
straddled addled adjectives, adverbs dragging
their butts. All unemployed and lonely.
Oh those helpless, hopeless shallow faces!

I demand the right
to love, hate, desire, fear, loathe,
wish for, believe, doubt, accept,
reject, honor, envy, assume and
question all at the same time.

Where is the emoji that says life is tragic?
That the lost stay stubbornly lost,
suddenly, impossibly gone, like bird wings,
their lines erased in the distant blue, leaving us

unable to prove our case.
Yet my time will come, you wait.
I will hide a book in every silence.
And when you read your soul will alight
like a firefly's lust at midnight.
You will remember the treasure you lost.

A note on B.S.: Although I will be documenting this text with vital footnotes, I refuse here to dignify this poem with my beautiful mind. This poem, to be blunt, is clearly and appallingly obscene. It is well that its author is anonymous, since he/she/they/us/you /everybody/nobody is clearly implying that those who make use of social media to share their expertise on everything that is happening to them in the immediate moment are *not really communicating*. This claim was especially irksome to the glorious Dr. Botkin, driving him at times to swat flies all day long. The falsity of this claim of non-communication is so patently absurd, that I have found only one literary critic—another Leslie Fiedler—who supports it, and the second Fiedler, it is commonly known, humiliated himself when he infamously and prematurely announced, not the death of the author, but the death of terminal alliteration. This was a tragic end for a once revered critic, whose mind became so filled with energy from reading the works of other critics that his head gradually grew too heavy for his neck to sustain, bowing over time closer and closer to the ground like a limb of the mighty oak that one day it fell to the ground like a ripe apple and began running about on its own in search of the Ur In-Text Citation. It is now commonly accepted among textual scholars that the first commentator to rely heavily on the internal footnote was Foster Delirious, who famously declared: "Give me an internal footnote and I will move the earth." Tragically, before he could move much earth, Dr. Delirious was skewered by a Pavlovian Hussar. However, luckily his copious knowledge of The Chicago Manual of Style was passed down through numerous copyright and plagiarism trials to his disciple, Dr. Terry Trismegistus. Dr. Trismegistus continued the tradition of the in-text citation throughout his life, which unfortunately was cut short. He died from an intestinal disturbance brought about by premature Epistasis.

## Invisible Narcissus

Wireless apocalypse,
a loneliness with sharp bright teeth,
alert as radar
to all incoming threats
yet longing for a single touch
to unfold you into light.

I am I this all alone
three hundred friends
I have never met.
Photo-shopped faces
with no need for masks.
You learn to read between the lies.

And I am the echo's echo,
my Narcissus nowhere to be seen,
alive, I guess, in my cave of glass.
We are all of us speaking in thumbs.

I long to tell my mother
every secret I hid between my words.
I long to tell a secret lover
how I am made of flesh and bone.

But my mother died
from terminal silence,
and my lover is a lie
I tell myself.

Sometimes I hear my own echo
tapping on the hull of a sunken ship,
hopelessly below all soundings.
A song that's learned to sing itself away.

## How to make *Oppenheimer* truly realistic

"A gripping tale of the complexity of history and the human character." —Four Star Review

But since complexity is filth,
let us proceed:

First, remove the exit signs and bar the doors.
Irradiate the popcorn so the watchers can feel
the inner glow of cinematic satisfaction.
Seed the Good & Plenty with plenty of good
blasting caps, especially recommended for those
adept at World War Two video games.
Announce there will be no coming attractions.

Ramp up the Surround-Sound to pure apocalypse
until their addicted eyeballs bulge and pop from their sockets.
Have the usher pass up and down each aisle,
flashing her light on each terrified consumer,
announcing they are serial killers in disguise.
Pump waves of charcoal dust over the congregation
until they become the stenciled ash of schoolchildren
drawn carefully on playground walls.

Let the screen go blank and black
until there is no end to darkness.

# Why no one remembers the name of Janet Leigh's character in *Psycho*

1
Conundrum the saint
with the sadness of Autumn crickets.
Flow your love to what cries unseen.

2
Rattle the linguist
with the voices of stones.
Render him soft as ashes.

3
Humble the poet,
death's ventriloquist.
Victim means knife stuck in throat.

4
Riddle the scholar a cliff of fall—
You must step through vertigo
to learn the meaning of a wound.

5
Man is a killer, the purest kind,
makes death an art,
kills first in his mind.

6

The hotel glows like Martian cancer.
The moon draws darkness to it,
the screen all mushroom, mushroom, mushroom.

7

Her part is pure pantomime.
She dies and dies without a why.
The dead speak the earth to silence.

# The killer

The killer cleaves a thought from reason
and casts it to bloody silence.
He dreams all pain his private aria,
and makes his violence an art.

The killer unravels day from night,
then speaks that night to horrors.
His every word wounds his victim,
who dies without a why.

The killer's love is carved from daggers.
He'll stab a witness moon.
He dreams each night of smothered doves,
and the earth beds all his lovers.

The killer is a visionary
who sees his fated doom
in a slouched hat and cigarette,
and a coin cut from the moon.

The killer dangles like Peter's wolf,
that swallows whole its victims.
But the bird perches high in safety,
singing all his sins.

## Regeneration through violence

A boy leads the old knight through the woods,
his armor rusted, his body scarred. He sings
as the boy lays him in the brown grass.
The air shudders, yet brings no rain.
The knight's eyes fade like forgotten battles.
Nothing was ever really won.

The boy bites his young wrists till they bleed,
then mingles his blood with the dying knight's.
Shadows bloom as the light slowly starves.
Birds descend to pluck his heart and liver.
Yet the knight feels nothing, immune to all pain.
He sings the names of the knights he has slain.

Now winds come unloving in the dawn.
The boy sings of future victories.
Not one note redeems the fallen.
He takes the sword lovingly in his hands,
studies it, eyes filling with battles,
in awe and dreaming of future kills.

# The Outcasts of Golgotha Heights

(Setting: A burial cave with a large rock poked in its entrance. Five men are playing cards on a stone slab. Three nineteenth century oil lamps provide light. Two whiskey bottles sit on the stone slab, along with the Holy Grail).

Ludwig Wittgenstein: Even a Verification Principle needs to be verified, since any logical proposition assumes its own logic.
Donald Trump: Still not listening.
(Eighteen badly-concealed cards are poking their heads out of various parts of his oversized suit).
Wittgenstein: I could not get the Logical Positivists to see the limits of logic. Spiritual truths cannot be spoken. They are within the silence, and that silence is holy.
Trump: Blah, blah, blah. Can we get back to talking about me?
Jesus Christ: What are Jacks worth again?
Trump: All right, I'll do it myself. Amazing. Tremendous. Bigley. Huge. China. China is huge. Bigley. Big water. Ocean water. Like nobody's seen before. Greater than Washington. Greater than Lincoln.
Jesus: Can't any of you gentlemen find some way to make this man stop talking?
Satan: Well I sure as Hell don't want him. If I ever dragged that fat carcass of gas to Hell with me, the legion of demons would excommunicate me. Besides, I'm draw towards a royal flush here. Oops.
Trump (Continuing): Enemies of the People. Bad. Sad. Badsad. Sadbad. Terrible. Horrible. Disgraceful. Quite frankly, a disgrace. Like nobody's ever seen before.
The Sundance Kid: Son, if you don't stop flapping your gums

soon, your mouth is gonna meet the wrong end of a Colt. 45.
Jesus: I can't seem to stop drawing bad hands. I'm gonna need a miracle here.
Satan: Nothing personal, wonderboy, but aren't you supposed to be daring Hell about now?
Jesus: Don't judge me. I've already been to Akron, isn't that enough?
(Overhead outside, two F-37 fighter jets crucify the sky with controlled terror).
Wittgenstein: I loathe those things. We have constructed a God-less world.
Trump: Who are these two Hebes? They sound un-American.
(Christ's cell phone plays "We Wish You a Merry Christmas.")
Jesus: Wait a sec. I gotta take this one.
Wittgenstein: Oh, now I'm drawing to a good hand. Still, one must not be proud. This is still a game which consists largely of chance. The only game that is only intelligence, imagination, memory and skill, is chess.
Sundance: You ain't winnin nothing if you don't stop announcing all your hands, pard.
Jesus (speaking on his phone): WHAT? What do you mean you can't move the rock? That's just an old philosopher's trick!
Satan: Good heavens! Why did you tell him about the Omnipotence Paradox? He'll be pondering on that one for centuries.
(A huge explosion outside, followed by machine gun fire).
Sundance: It sure sounds like The good Old West out there, but I don't remember any cave with a rock stuck in it anywhere near Hole in the Wall.
Trump (in panic). Hole in the wall! Where?
Satan: It could be the apostles trying to break in.
Jesus: Do you mind? I'm on long distance here.
Satan: Spending all that time lepers and poor people, you must really suffer from FOMO.
(Another explosion. The ground shakes).

There goes another one. You guys are really making this too easy for me.

Jesus: It's not my fault. Climate change melted both ice poles and there's been a shift in the earth's magnetic field. It seems that all wars are melding into one giant war out there.

Satan: Really? Goody! A total clusterfuck!

Jesus: You're telling me. There may BE no resurrection. We may have to use this cave as a bomb shelter.

Trump: Climate change? That's from China, right? China's a huge country. Nobody knows how huge. Nobody knows there's millions and millions and billions and billions of Chinamen.

Sundance: Where the hell did you find him?

Wittgenstein: None of this is turning out the way I had hoped.

Trump: You're telling me. Bust! Bust? I can't go bust!

Satan: Nonsense. You've gone bust six times already.

Trump: I never lose. This game is rigged! I'm the greatest man who ever lived.

Wittgenstein: You are nothing but a pack of cards.

Jesus: How are we ever going to move that rock out of the way? Woe on those Romans and their cursed building skills. Rats! Now the line's gone dead.

Satan: Strange. I would have thought that the God of the Catholic Church would have a mass audience.

Jesus: Ha-ha. Father always said you had a good sense of humor.

Satan: Nothing like his.

Sundance: Hey, I just picked a great card. Damn! Now you've got me doing it!

Jesus: Jesus, we may be stuck in here three whole days!

Sundance: In that case, you'd better break out more whiskey.

Wittgenstein: We finished the whiskey an hour ago.

Sundance: All right, so send over that bottle of wine.

Wittgenstein: You finished that off an hour ago.

Jesus: Wait—wait a minute—You drank the wine?

Sundance: Sure did, pard.

Jesus: The wine on the table?

Sundance: Yeah, the stuff in that strange looking bottle there.

Jesus: Oh my god, I don't believe...YOU DRANK THE EUCHARIST!

Sundance: I did? Damn. I wondered why it had such a kick.

Jesus: Please don't take this the wrong way, but I was saving that for a very special occasion.

Wittgenstein: Draw a picture of a car accident. The picture points to the event, establishes a relation in the mind. This establishes reality. This was my old viewpoint. My new viewpoint? Now draw a picture of an ambulance, because you're going to need it.

Sundance (Pondering): Oh. Oh! Listen, I didn't know. I just figured with no food, the drinks were on the house.

(Sundance spreads his card hand across the table like a peacock spreading its feathers).

Sundance: Ah ha! Gin!

(A gigantic explosion overhead).

Satan: I thought we were playing poker. No wonder I've been losing.

Wittgenstein: My God, will this war never end?

Satan: Listen, Jesus, I can get you a sweet deal on some killer drones if you want. That way the good guys can win, whoever the hell they are.

Jesus: No one ever wins a war. Everyone loses. The war alone wins—always.

(Another explosion outside, followed by machine gun fire. Lights down).

# There is a suffering inner far

There is a suffering inner far
than galaxies fathom their stars
to mystery, an electricity
through the veins,
which sparks to a pain, an outrage,
and stuns you from sleep with a scream.

It is a savage algebra,
indifferent as division,
impatient as an X.
Won't scare, scar over,
won't leave the scene of a crime
it refuses to unsee.

A hieroglyph of wounds
scrawled on the darkness,
it cannot speak its name,
but you will know it when it comes.
It will stun you to a silence,
and rattle you bone by bone.

## Prayer to someone listening

This world they want us to believe in
is blind, deranged, and self-destructive,
or perhaps the opposite,
a bold bright light of insanity
that sees only itself.
Like the night-flames of a Nazi death camp
illuminating the void.

What psychiatrists fail to see
is that the mind suffers alone,
knows this world is mad
yet still unfurls into itself,
fearing there is no other tapestry to weave.
Yet the pain this world imagines
imagines through blood and bone.

God keep me this side the cliffs of fall,
that I may somehow climb to reason,
and if that fails, a faith may do,
in some world the dead never dreamed.

## The world as wound and vision

A Winter mind can wither any sunrise,
December branches crucified in stars.
An Autumn wind bursts in bloodstained whispers,
and sends its moons in secret through your veins.

The pirate mind hears clocks in crocodiles.
All your fears are pinned on thorns of stars.
Hunger crows come bruising every windstorm.
Save yourself by counting down your bones.

The cross-winged sun of furious Summer
burns its ashes deep within your lungs.
Hold your breath to learn what winds may know.
Shatter the mirror to get the world back clean.

Then let Spring come iffing through the grass.
Your blood is blooming roses through the air.
Let tears and rain fall in old devotions.
Bite your wrist to drink the dreaming there.

## Theophany in City Park

Voices of children are cupped in leaves,
and carried tree to tree.
Perhaps heaven is a foreign land
hidden within our own.
Like a whisper in the blood,
a still, quiet voice in bright colors.
Perhaps God is his own confession.

Perhaps the mind alone is master,
and this whole park a revelation,
and here, where families spread their picnics,
answers may come whirling round as leaves.

I come here alone, to seek forgotten clues,
my past gone far down sledded hills,
searching for something I thought I once knew,
a thought bright and fading as the moon.

## Watching a picnic

The sun is resisting clichés again.
The clouds are ballerinas,
the picnic lawn delirious in green.
But I am the staying bird of snows.

They move like a raveling spool of sparrows
around the healthy table.
I am just here. They smile, hug, laugh and shout.
How easeful if their opening to love.

I two-finger a smile towards heaven—
trying—My fingers drop—
failure to launch, no faking.
They eye the sunny food with joy.

I don't dislike them. I long to say:
"Look! I'm so happy I'm delicious!
Eat me and be well." But their hearts
are heliotrope, mine is all blue moon.

What if they did invite this stranger?
What speaking could I be? I'd as well
carve my heart as carve their beast.
I watch the leaves, trying to pull free.

I hear the winds themselves,
trying too hard to say.

## Moonlight relation

Watch this moon,
its half-closed eye of a sly black cat.
Watch its light as it gifts you vision,
its gentle, persistent silence
felt along your breath
and deep within your bones,
moonlight within the purr of darkness,
moonlight's perfection of alone.
Now look. It has rounded to a full.
No longer mother, her child in her arms,
but pure huntress, bending time with her bow,
drawing your passion with perfect aim.

# Chandelier moon

The sun rises.
The chandelier lights to honeycomb.

Later, the moon arrives,
and gently undresses her wealth.

## Out of the web to weaving

Everyone is watching everyone.
Not good, not healthy, not kind.
So follow these footsteps and say no more,
and we'll go somewhere inner far
than the rose bled down to center earth.
Then rise again
through every branch and leaf of longing,
speaking to the winds.

The poem is sure, knows where it's heading.
Trust the line it traces like a diamond
tracing its signature down a stone,
and every word a diamond
compressing into truth.

Stray us then through all desire,
a covenant of interlocking bodies,
our love an incarnation in the grass,
until we find the secret place
where no one is alone.

# The tenacity of silence

Silence, like a fossil leaf,
etches itself in time.,
oozes to a center,
clings to sudden light.
Moves with mastered grace
like a magician's wand,
a mystery, a discipline,
practicing its art.
Smooths the stones
to calm the earth,
curves to a sweet embrace,
weaves bone to bone,
binding us to the real.
Secret, prefers the touch
of flesh to any vow.
Patient, awaits its chance
to fall between drops of rain.
Sometimes, if you listen,
it's been known to unfold a world.

# Holy in silence

Holy in silence, the leaves await the storm.
Holy the moon, the host raised to silence
while shadows hide their whispers from the light.
Silence, the thief of reason, silence,
a child that awakes unseen.

Not for us the ignorant winds
that rage the sky to wounds,
nor the arrogant sun who struts his knowings.
Silence, the lure of the shy deer's beauty,
since, the art of waiting.

Holy the silence of the firefly's gift
that sutures the night with gold.
And holy the silence of the patient graves
that bind the earth to memory.
When silence listens, love battens on the real.

# Tree sermon

I spoke a sermon to a tree.
It did not interrupt.
It did not sulk or talk back.

It never once ignored me,
shifted root, or changed
to judge and jury.

It did not budge a bud or leaf
for me or my bustling words.
It did not hate.

My symbols slipped from twig to twig.
Not one took hold, my summation
cast to the winds.

When I was done, I felt pure,
and the tree went right on treeing.
Dreaming, perhaps, of silence.

## Tree of hearts

Synchronized osmosis.
Trees have heartbeats,
the water pumped in sudden waves
from root to trunk to branch,
at night, when all the secrets flow.

The Chamber of Commerce collapsed in terror
to learn the world's currency
runs not on money but in rivers.
The scientists fainted from the thrill of their finding.
Though we with bloodhearts can't see why.

If everything's alive and drawn to moontide,
prescient, aware of its own mortal pulse,
then the whole world is suffering with itself.
The tree knows the swinging blade will end it,
and leaves shiver with their only freedom.

We will need to step more carefully now
that every breath comes wounding all this green.

## The wren of heaven

This wren contains a light it cannot see.
I see it.  It perches in her song.
Yet I am darkness, incapable of flight.
Her song is incandescent, yet a song
alone because I hear it.

She sings and sings, her song unwinding time.
How blessed and lost she seems,
to be in heaven without her knowing,
while I'm in hell because I long for God.

# Atalanta

Parhelion butterfly
kaleidoscopes the dawn,
tracing eminiscates in the light.
An acrobat of the merest breeze,
with no need for net.

Its iridescent wings hover,
then ride a gentle wind from tree to tree,
its versipel light unknown to the nooning sun
unveiling carillon colors of the new.

It floats from shade to shade,
flower to flower, sun to moon,
then, before it comes to rest
on a timid blade of grass,
autographs the sky in silent pride.

# Mr. Shade's redemption

He steps inside the shadow of a gull
and leaves the earth for a timeless breath.
A black wing guides him through a wind,
and now whole wheels of them descend,
weaving the air with light.
He steps from earth through a door in the air,
and all is well, as if this fountain of birds
were a dance of random angels biding time.

And he is free and whole for now,
as if chess pawns, briefly weightless,
are leaping nights and moons to ripen
into queens, and sometimes
in the midst of whirling cries of hunger,
and the chaos of lonely gales,
his words and they worlds they play
suddenly come aright.

(A)

A. Far be it for me to compete with Professor Shade in the precise art of footnoting, but I do wish here to note his curious obsession with this poem. He repeatedly insisted I censor it, since he believed it was an intentional broadside aimed at him by an anonymous person working as part of an anti-Shade conspiracy. This of course completely contradicts his earlier claim to me that all the poems in the book were secret homages to himself. Still, I agreed to his demands initially, but now that Shade has apparently disappeared, I see no reason not to print it. I repeatedly tried, to no avail, to assure Dr. Shade that the author of this piece most likely did not even know who he -Shade- was, but this attempt at assuagement only seemed to drive him into a fiercer fury. As evidence for the commonsense justness of my viewpoint, I would like to point out that I randomly chose a town phone directory on the internet, Cloudcuck, Montana, to test the validity of my reassurance to Dr. Shade. Sure enough, this phonebook lists 4,599 residents, of which 4,598 are named Botkin Shade.

My only regret now is that I was never able to share this remarkable finding with the good doctor. I can't help but feel that somehow it would soothe his sensitive nerves to learn that his name is as well-known and popular as "John Smith" or Scot Towels.

Internal footnote: The perspicuous reader may have noted that in this footnote I employ a letter (A) in place of the traditional number. In all modesty, I consider this a significant innovation in the art of footnoting, and plan to have it copyrighted soon. This latter step has proven necessary due to the egregious practice by some of my more ambitious colleagues of *borrowing* (read stealing) my innovation, without proper citation or payment. Never let it be said, however, that life lacks poetic justice. The same perceptive reader complimented above may also note that, while the potential number of numbers is theoretically without limit, there are, sadly, a mere twenty-seven letters in our alphabet, twenty-six if one counts the "w" as unoriginal, a mere amalgam of two "u's." This begs the philosophical question of what the enterprising scholar is to do when he runs out of letters with which to develop his textual commentaries. This publisher/editor, if I may confess to a confessional mode, is immodest enough to admit a secret glee in reporting that this dilemma has led to a number of suicides among my colleagues (enemies) when they came to the end of the line, so to speak, without any means of guiding the reader to the all-important footnote. I hope my loving reader will not pass judgement upon me for this, since I consider it no sin to spread hopelessness and despair among the terminally ambitious, spiteful, and confused. The reduction in population of literary critics can only raise the quality of the gene pool.

# The complicity of explanation

—to Botkin Shade (B)

Now blood in your palms is screaming.
Now mandrake cries are riven down your spine.
You shall not shall not dream an explanation,
nor be granted pardon from a why,
when barbed wire tongues string from death to silence.

The crime forms first within the mind.
The blood burns long before the wound.
and daggers come dreaming up the walls
long before the raven croaks an entrance,
long before your mirrors embrace your doom.

Guilt seeps deep as fog into the bone.
And words are things, blind as any stone.
You do not know your own soliloquy.
An atrocity of ghosts and snowflake ashes
comes to bless the city of the dead.

Now you are different from what you are.
Now you are another of another,
the darkest angels flowing from your orphan,
the wounds of trauma carved within your arm.
Agony cries our kinship with the dust.

(B) I am aware that this may seem anomalous, but Dr. Shade repeatedly (and furiously, to be honest) denied to me that this poem was in any way related to himself. He insisted, instead, that it refers to *another* Botkin Shade, and that this other Botkin Shade had been following him everywhere, doing impersonations of him. Shade (The original Shade, that is) claimed that the line, "Now you are another of another" is in fact an allusion to this malignant impersonator. This, the good doctor claimed, is merely a hazard of his profession, ie: so many other scholars had for so many years imitated his style, borrowed his research without request, and even plagiarized some of his most beloved lines, that it was inevitable that one of them would attempt to plagiarize him body and soul, turn into him, or at least into a simulacrum of him, and in fact, might HAVE turned into him, or at least another him, a kind of secret sharer of divine knowledge. If this is true, then the kind professor deserves all sympathy, and the potential consequences for academia seem grave indeed. I am not, mind you, giving full credence to his theory as of yet, though I have begun to double-track my own steps, at times, just to make certain that I do not have an impersonator following me, making faces purporting to be my own. So far I am proud to report my utterly solitary state of being. Still, sometimes late, during the odd bent hours of the night, on the far reaches of my short-wave radio, I suspect I hear the distant laptop typing of a madman, attempting to duplicate me as I drift off to sleep.

—R.S.R.

## What the night sky knows

It darkness draws the nearing stars
around every human dream,
weaving its black heaven
from light to light.
Some nights,
a single cricket call
makes it shimmer, shimmer…
and now the stars bead a knife blade
suspended in the pines.
Words, mere pebbles,
sink through its endlessness,
while sea clouds,
spiraling into doves,
capture the moon.

## Do stars remember beyond their light?

What memory draws stars to shining?
The heart searches night for origins.
A high election guides the longing eye,
seeking angels dying into breath.

Your stare moves through these lyres of silence,
and turning spheres of distant, pulsing bliss.
How many worlds far beyond yourself
lie awake to your undreaming?

The depths between them darken your desire.
Mystical cobwebs, candlebloom, and you.
Swing your vision from these chandeliers,
all this darkness speaking into light.

Then tell of all you saw in your alone.

## Some Devout haiku

Why are you here?
Zebra night
snowfall.

2/3/74
the lights
began

Ubique
satori—
look sharp

Witness
the purloined
divinity

Any lost object
may be the holy grail,
any lost person the Buddha

No fish
with guns
allowed

Waste
the silent
empire

The word
finally free
from the net
(C)

(A) Editor's explanation: In a series of text messages to me before he disappeared from the internet and quite possibly from reality, Dr. Shade insisted that all these poems must have originated from the same writer. I am not certain I agree, but his argument is compelling, especially if one gives credence to Shade's theory that numerous writers have been engaging in the process of impersonating one another. Shade claimed that these are a series of haiku, a poetry form whose brevity fits well with text messaging, but whose apparent complexity does not. He traced some allusions to the works of Philip K. Dick, a known lunatic, and also to several novels by Thomas Pynchon, a notorious liberal whose refusal to use social media has led some to claim that he is a dangerous anarchist or may, conversely, not exist at all. The poems appear to have been written in code, perhaps decipherable only by the Devout, who must consider themselves to be some form of cognoscenti. This, of course, is a vicious lie, since every literary critic knows that the poet is deaf and dumb without a literary critic to explicate them. If the poems are written in code, such elitism is distasteful although it might show some potential for those scholars seeking tenure or promotion. The reference to "satori" appears to be taken from the works of another lunatic, D.T. Suzuki, a man whose first two initials obviously show him to have been a raging alcoholic. According to my best internet sources, a satori is a divine revelation of the holiness of life, one that can occur anywhere, and at any time, to any one person. That smells of democracy, not to mention east coast liberal high-mindedness. It is certainly NOT in any way similar to Christian divine grace of the Puritan variety, since this experience, far from being available to anyone, is reserved for the Elect. The rest live in terminal darkness similar to those who do not own smartphones. Between these two Weltenschung, I much prefer the latter, since it fits neatly into my own perceptions and experience. I am clearly full of Grace, and eagerly await the day when I am raptured out of my clothes in public.

## The poem

The poem worm
digs
towards the body of its hunger.

The poem,
a mole,
evades the explanations of the sun.

The poem snake
hithers and slithers to its hole,
seeking the core of sweetness.

The poem lives
by threading the earth.
Inner earth, compressed to diamonds,
sings.

# Live to

Live to the constellations in your veins,
the roses singing in your blood,
until you hear the god of distant summers.

Live to your apprenticeship of dust,
that taught you light is woven from darkness,
then carried by ravens from suns to moons.

Unlock the light inside each stone,
then step through a doorway in the wind
and ghost your scriptures on the sky.

Hear the cries of the wound-forged meteors
then dance your way clear to a vision.
Count each seed full gently through the earth.

(D)

(B) Botkin claimed to have successfully traced this specific poem to one M. Schrift, going so far as to demand a Guggenheim grant in reward for his discovery. However, this publisher-turned-editor has diligently researched this claim and can find no merit in it. The good professor, usually quite detailed in his literary attributions, oddly never provided a source for his bold claim. And yes, dear reader, the man referred to here was INDEED the late, great classical scholar, Makeshift Schrift, discoverer of the internal footnote, who was tragically trampled to death by a herd of barking cats while attempting to teach a horse to speak Latin.

## Harold in a moment of supreme friction

While walking through my more or less,
used to unsurprised,
I met a man of many devices,
with pied coat and grinning harmonica,
who was juggling three greenblue balls
in happytragic arcs that caught the sun,
while writing something secret on his palm
in his own blood.

"How do you live?" I asked.

"I live anyway," he replied,
balancing a blue guitar on one foot.
He removed a glass eye and it winked at me.
Had he come to judge the world with laughter?

When I tried to laugh,
the choice shot two teeth from
my mouth like dice from a cop's slap.

"But why write on yourself?"

"Who else? Fable cool hot sidewalks."

With one hand he halted taxicabs of the abyss,
and offered me a ride outside the world,
sighed at my decline, then tunneled the post office,
signing his name to the letters of strangers.

"Robbing the divinity," he grinned.
Then he molded his face into those
of a thousand strangers.
In a few moments he'd impersonated half the town.

"Risking my insurance."

He shrugged his shoulders the way
Buddy Holly pushes up his glasses,
then leapt into a cloud,
laughing wicked rains.

I walked home, strangely soothed,
and happy for this rain with no umbrella. (E)

(E) Dr. Shade insisted to me many times, with a rage so intense that it drove him to giggling, that this poem is obscene. I concede that for a long while I had no idea what he was so angry about, but now I concur with his evaluation. My error was simple: I was looking only for what was there in the poem, and not at what was NOT there in the poem. Being by far the more experienced explicator of literary texts, Dr. Shade understood as I did not that perhaps the greatest contribution made to culture by literary critics is their remarkable ability to see things in a poet's work that are in fact not there at all. And what is missing from this poem that should, in fact, be there? Smartphones! Neither the poet nor the other strange person depicted in this poem are ever shown speaking into a phone or sending a text message while ignoring what's around them, behaviors that I hope my reader sees are clearly unnatural. While the old fashioned method of rhetoric allowed people to openly discuss issues in a friendly manner, the new "Twitterspeak" provides them with the much more satisfying opportunity to rage at each other without mercy or limit, thus providing the rager with the divine "high" of feeling forever noble, outraged, and righteous. The superiority of this newer form of communication over the old, outmoded and merely human one will appear obvious to anyone with even a minimum of four or five hundred internet friends and perhaps several thousand internet enemies. Shade insisted also that the poem might be an extended metaphor of his own Dickensian childhood, when he was forced to endure several months without any access to the internet or social media. Of course this assertion appears to contradict his earlier assertion that the poem is obscene. However, Shade declared that this was, in fact, "a poetic strategy" constructed on a series of "structural tensions," leading to an "apotheosis of paradox and irony" that molds the poem into "a pure cognitive object purged of all superfluous emotion." In other words, the poem was written by a thinking stone.

## Why my hero is an unhinged door

A hole so deep
it falls through itself.
In a land emoji,
a sad mind is handed a judgement.

"He's simply not normal,"
says the six-armed, eighteen-eyed
space alien to my long-dead mother,
who knew.

"He's guilty as charged,"
testifies Larry the secretive spy-bat.
"You wouldn't believe the things he thinks up
in the dark of his sleepless nights."

"La maudits," shrugs my lawyer,
demands verdict before trial.
"Your honor, my client pleads sanity,"
I say to twenty-four deaf ears.

If you've never been in a psyche ward here we go.
They strap you into a wheelchair like that guy in Rear Window,
enter you in a soap box derby down an underground tunnel
with a cop alongside who won't speak to or look at you. Yeah.

Shove you in a freight elevator, sight unseen,
You are now a criminal of the invisible.
Store you in a room with some stranger
who might be even stranger than you.

Lashed and makeshift,
my mental lifeboat would sink in a bathtub.
Doctors made of laptops and glasses
testify: "Resents authority of any kind."
"Unretractable." "Likes to be off by himself."
"Refuses to access the internet." "Claims to be born
from a non-virgin." "Tried to replace The Ten Commandments
with Ten Amendments." "Claims to be both fox and hedgehog."

True. My stencil mind
forever questions the patterns it makes.
Suspects this "real world"
is mere paper mache.

So they poke and probe and glib and frighten
and Freud me. Shock and rock and drug and drain me.
Then send me out blinking in sunlight,
found guilty of being born.

(F)

F. It might perhaps not come as a surprise to the reader by now that the at times seemingly stubborn professor Botkin also claimed that this poem is about himself. It appears that Dr. B's remarkable ability to empathize with others, combined with his intense close readings, caused him at times to, in effect, fall inside a poem like a cat falling into a well, to such a depth that he experienced difficulty finding his way back out. In this particular case, Botkin insists this poem refers to one of his apparently numerous stays in mental wards, citing as evidence that the words "stencil mind" refer to one of his psychiatrists, a Dr. W. Benway, known for his method of diagnosing his patients through the use of construction paper stencils. However, this diligent researcher was able to uncover the fact that Dr. W. Benway died in 1955 from terminal self-psychoanalysis. The only other Dr. Benway I could identify was Dr. B. Benway, an obscure scholar of the posthumous works of Henry James. B. Benway would be a questionable source for Dr. Botkin's claim, however, since not only was he not a practicing psychiatrist but he also allegedly once told police that he was being chased through airport terminals by a loose baggy monster. Moreover, Dr. B. Benway also once staked the dubious claim that he could play Beethoven's entire Ninth Symphony on his nose. Finally, it appears that Dr. B. Benway is also, at least currently, deceased. It seems that he perished in a freak accident. He was chasing an obscure footnote when he was run over by a freak.

# The man made of kite strings

I was making castles appear,
disappear, the sun my magic wand—
a cloud, a pebble, and puddle rings
wandering towards invisible constellations.

A man appeared, free and wondering,
kite-thin and wound-round with strings,
blooming above him kites of millioned colors,
like gentle eyes watching all the world.

He must have dreamed of painted butterflies.
He woke new patterns with his strings—
moon-to-moon, night-to-day, and more—
guided birds to stars, planets to new orbits.

Strangers danced together like puppets,
spiders webbed the sky with suns
towns, woods, rivers, seas, countries
bound each to each with string.

But with a pair of silver scissors
sharpened with pain, he cut the kite strings
all, and I fell through time and memory,
clutching at colors turned to distance.

"Why?" I cried. "Now I'm alone forever."
"Because," he whisper-sighed,
"We must all be connected
with strings we cannot see."

# Heaven-haven star to sea

Heaven-haven star to sea,
and winds of all my leavings,
when trees release their memories to Fall
I long for the other side of words
And still your name comes hidden in the rain.

The sun may cast its shadows on the dead,
and the night, dark angel,
fall eternal into silence
so pure, I hear a worm's dark windings.
And still your ghost waits gently in my bones.

Who were you, weaving stars to meanings?
And who am I then, and who am I now,
and how was I deserving your coming
to bloom my every night with seas and moon?
And still your love beats madly through my veins.

# Make it new

The elder trunks are wrapped in gentle baize.
Here we find the silence the grass keeps,
memory underground tracing roots of love.
Here we find sacred darkness,
where we learn touch and tongue,
eyes flowering to worlds we've never seen,
winds chanting our blood to secrets,
a madness for heights, felt along the wing,
rapt in curve and cry and call of joy.

Perhaps we end.
Perhaps we thread the endless constellations.

## The everyday randomness of grace

A young couple is running in a snowfall.
The flakes are large and descend as gently
as cabbage moths
or the moon broken into countless memories.

She cradles a package like a football
and races past him, laughing
in the sun's frozen watching,
her dark hair a moment in the wind

the wind a sudden embrace.
She laterals the package to him
and guides him through leaping opponents
towards the post office spun to emerald.

They are lovers with a message, a gift
to be sent hand-to-hand of strangers
a trust along with thousands of others,
sent to a world of possibilities.

They return arm-in-arm, heads bowed,
whispering secrets in the diamond air,
knowing sometimes mere contingency
is all the heaven we need.

# Death is a bad mechanic

Old age is the only expensive car I ever bought,
in the foolish hope it would last my remaining days.
Then one day go to make a U-turn
and the damn steering wheel pulls off in my hands.
Time resents U-turns as a general rule,
and steer-less roads are uncooperative.

Then my best tire blows, and my brother is gone
before his time, the driver's door, my best friend
in an emergency, pulls away like it wants to fly.
Now the back tires go, my mother and father with them.
My last tire complains suspiciously like me
and the rear-view mirror won't stop weeping.

My only map is a tangle of arteries and veins
that seem to lead everywhere and nowhere,
the clutch becomes my aorta
and jams like a really bad rock band,
and now my mind is all on the engine,
praying it won't stop or stall.

This is when I find religion again,
in a new incarnation of fear,
the radio blubbering God, please no,
not now, not here, this is too ridiculous
a way to go, can't I just explode?
Goddamn you, God, is this your sense of humor?

And I dream of my Matchbox car racetrack
I made on my mother's dining room table,
with chalk for lines and a wet rag for smooth lanes,
the cars calmly aligned, with rules and pit stops
for repairs, no one died, victory was ever near,
and the world turned forever round and round.

## A country store

My grandmother's antique store
preserves the past in rows of fragile glass.
Sunlight touches them red to gold,
the moon to blue and silver,
transforming all the world.

Such a curious word—antique—
since this room's all alive to me.
The clocks that round the walls,
each hand a moment lost long ago.
A spinning wheel that threads the night with stars,
a flintlock cocked at an invisible foe,
and a Civil War bullet
pried from flesh and bone.

These are the echoes of human lives
that shimmer through my veins.
Sometimes I hear their ghosting footsteps
pacing the midnight's creaking floors.

Yet for all this loneliness and pain,
I choose this pane of many-colored glass
over the pale white radiance of eternity.

# Why I am old and I guess it's all right

1
Because I still await
the final lesson.

2
Because I have learned to write
from the body to the mind

3
Because it is just possible
I have learned how to listen.

4
Because the stars are at last a mystery
I do not need to solve.

5
Because pauses between winds
know more than any word.

6
Because everything is carcinogenic,
so stop worrying.

7
Because there is less lust, more laughter,
but still some lust.

8
Because old wounds
died first.

9
Because it was probably all my fault
and I can still breathe.

10
Because I am no longer afraid
to call the dead my own.

Bookseller's Final Note

It is with deepest regret that I now must bid my reader adieu. It appears someone has stolen my identity and has used it to purchase my own house and evict me. Moreover, this new Sanctus is actually claiming to be me on my website, and is collecting all royalties, illegally, from earlier Laputa Press books. He is even claiming to be the true author of *The Secret History of the Origin of Everything* and of both professor Shade's and my own unique and invaluable commentaries. Not only that, but he has sued me in open court for full publication rights, and appears to be winning. He is utterly shameless but highly skilled, able to shift from one identity to another with the ease of clicking on a new emoji. I blame society. We are pressured to such an egregious degree to create internet profiles so hopelessly out of touch with reality and our actual selves that apparently someone became so envious of my autobiography that they simply pilfered it for their own subversive use. Far be it for me to in any way condone the ideas of horrid little Nietzsche, but he did write one fully wise line, and perhaps I might best close with it: "Become what you are."

Rich Sanctus (former)

www.ingramcontent.com/pod-product-compliance
Lightning Source LLC
LaVergne TN
LVHW041044150826
845672LV00001B/465

* 9 7 8 8 1 1 9 6 5 4 1 4 7 *